TWELVE MORE LADIES

GOOD, BAD AND INDIFFERENT

TWELVE MORE LADIES:

GOOD, BAD AND INDIFFERENT

By SIDNEY DARK

Essay Index Reprint Series

BOOKS FOR LIBRARIES PRESS
FREEPORT, NEW YORK

First Published 1932
Reprinted 1969

STANDARD BOOK NUMBER:
8369-1177-6

LIBRARY OF CONGRESS CATALOG CARD NUMBER:
70-86744

PRINTED IN THE UNITED STATES OF AMERICA

CONTENTS

CONTENTS

THE twelve ladies of this volume are a more mixed bag than those of my *Twelve Great Ladies*. My original intention was to select twelve ladies, conspicuous for masterfulness, and ten of my twelve were certainly masterful. The other two crept in by sheer caprice, Queen Philippa because she is one of the most attractive figures of the later Middle Ages, and Nell Gwynne mainly because she is so extremely good to write about. In a sense, each of my ladies was a conqueror. Even Queen Philippa saved the burghers of Calais and introduced rosemary into English gardens, two considerable achievements. Cleopatra failed in the end. Nell Gwynne died in comparative poverty. Napoleon's mother saw the tragedy of St. Helena as well as the glory of the Tuileries. But each of the three, according to their varying ambitions, had a tremendous run before the end. The others all had their heart's desire, though sometimes, as in the case of St. Joan, paying a heavy price for it.

I have written of Elizabeth before and at far greater length, but she is perhaps the most master-

ful woman in history, and in the brief sketch of her
here I have been concerned only with two phases of
an amazing character. The first is the success
with which she used a possible marriage as a counter
in the tricky diplomacy of her reign, never for one
moment intending to marry. And the second is
that she never was a Protestant in the sense that
Luther and Calvin were Protestant and that Dr.
Barnes is a Protestant today. She belonged to that
considerable class that has lived in every century,
the Catholic agnostics, and she was forced by
political necessity into an antagonism with the
Papacy. It may seem something of an imperti-
nence to write of Queen Elizabeth's later years
after Mr. Lytton Strachey's inimitable study, but
my second point is largely ignored by Mr. Strachey,
who, I take it, if he had to choose, would prefer
Geneva to Rome. The same explanation applies to
the inclusion of my sketch of Florence Nightingale,
the writing of which has been made easy by the
recent publication of Miss Irene Cooper Willis's
admirable biography. What is to me the chief
interest in Miss Nightingale is the difference in
character and methods that distinguishes her from
that other great woman reformer, St. Teresa.

I have been impressed by the fact that most of
these women, who in one way or another played

their part in history, have been rebels against family restriction and family tradition, a disconcerting discovery to one who believes that the family is the basis of civilisation, and a curious confirmation of the theories set out years ago by Mr. Bernard Shaw in his *Quintessence of Ibsenism.* Elizabeth was by no means indifferent to " the pull of the family," but she conquered it and sent her cousin to the block. St. Joan, St. Teresa, and Florence Nightingale were active rebels against the family. The only women with whom I have been concerned who can be correctly described as " family women " are Queen Philippa and Mme. Bonaparte, the mother of Napoleon, and it may well be believed that if Napoleon could have forgotten his family, he would have died Emperor of the French. Mrs. Booth was an admirable wife and mother, but her mission was as completely the first consideration of her life as it was of the brief and glorious life of St. Joan.

That I may not be chided for not doing what I have had no intention of doing, I would repeat that in this book, as in my other historical sketches, I have written for a public neither scholarly nor sophisticated, but with an intelligent curiosity to know something of the history of the past. With this in mind, I have selected interesting and typical figures incidentally to suggest the significance of the ages in which they have lived. If I succeed, to some small extent, in adding to understanding and in affording some measure of entertainment to the considerable number of readers for whom it has been my privilege to write for what has become, alas, a long number of years, I shall be more than satisfied.

SIDNEY DARK.

CLEOPATRA

ON a spring day in the year 41 B.C., Mark Antony, one of the Triumvirs who, since the assassination of Julius Cæsar three years before, had ruled the Roman world was, with his numerous suite, waiting impatiently on the quay-side at Tarsus, the city of Cilicia in the south of Asia Minor, important at the time as a seaport and as the terminus of the road across Mount Taurus, and remembered in these days as the birthplace of St. Paul. Mark Antony was then a man of forty-two, with a hook nose, low forehead and flowing beard, a man of pleasant humour and courteous manner, popular with his soldiers as his master Cæsar had been, fond enough of intrigue, but soldier rather than statesman, hot-headed, improvident, ostentatious but not uncultured, with a fatal tendency to periods of laziness and inertia after hectic bouts of activity—and always the easy slave of women. He was waiting for the beginning of what Anatole France has called " the maddest and most terrible of love stories."

Antony was waiting for Cleopatra. Cleopatra was the last of the Ptolemies, the descendants of one of Alexander the Great's most trusted soldiers, who was with the Macedonian in his conquest of India and became Satrap of Egypt after the conqueror's death in 323 B.C. The Ptolemies reigned in Egypt for nearly three hundred years. They were Greeks, and they remained Greek. The city which Alexander founded was a Greek city, and the civilisation of Egypt was Greek civilisation tempered, materialised and vulgarised by wealth. The character of the Egypt of Cleopatra was entirely different from the character of the country in the years that had seen the construction of the Pyramids and the Sphinx. Cleopatra has been rhetorically described as " the serpent of old Nile." As a matter of fact she was a cultured Greek lady, subtle-minded, unmoral, extremely gifted, in many respects, in her charm and her talent as in her incapacity to resist the maddest of passions, an anticipation of Mary, Queen of Scots.

Seven years before Antony impatiently awaited her on the quay at Tarsus, Cleopatra, then a girl of twenty, had enslaved Julius Cæsar. Cæsar had gone to Alexandria, after the death of his rival Pompey, and had established a Roman dictatorship in Egypt. Cleopatra and her brother, who in the

manner of the Ptolemies was also her husband,
were rivals for the Egyptian throne, and Cleopatra
had decided that to secure her sovereignty she
must contrive a personal interview with Cæsar and
win him to her cause by her charm. Plutarch has
described how the interview was arranged:

"Cleopatra, taking Apollodorus the Sicilian
alone of all her friends with her, and getting into a
small boat, approached the palace as it was growing
dark; and as it was impossible for her to escape
notice in any other way, she got into a bed sack
and laid herself out at full length, and Apollodorus,
tying the sack together with a cord, carried her
through the doors to Cæsar. Cæsar is said to have
been first captivated by this device of Cleopatra,
which showed a daring temper, and being completely enslaved by his intercourse with her and her
attractions, he brought about an accommodation
between Cleopatra and her brother on the terms
of her being associated with him in the kingdom."

From the fact that she could be thus carried in a
"bed sack," even though it was capacious, it has
been assumed that Cleopatra was slender and
dainty, but, according to contemporary writers, it
was her supreme grace rather than her regular
beauty that was her chief possession   I again
quote Plutarch:

" Her beauty alone was not so incomparable that
there could not have been other women as beautiful
as she; nor was it such that she incontinently
ravished all those that looked upon her; but her
converse, to those that frequented her, was so
agreeable that it was impossible to avoid being
captivated thereby; and with her beauty, the good
grace with which she conversed and the sweetness
and gentleness of her disposition, which gave a
fragrance to all that she said or did, was a thorn
that pierced to the quick; and it was, apart from
this, a great pleasure to hear merely the sound of
her voice and her manner of utterance, for her
tongue was as an instrument of music of many stops
and registers, which she employed readily in any
language that it pleased her to speak; so that she
seldom spoke with barbarous peoples through an
interpreter but replied to them herself, or at least
to the greater number of them, as the Egyptians,
Arabs, Troglodytes, Hebrews, Syrians, Medes and
Parthians, and to many others whose tongues she
had learned."

When Cæsar landed in Alexandria the city was
far more cultured than Rome. It possessed its
famous library of five hundred thousand MSS. It
was the home of scholars as well as of successful
traders. But the Alexandrine Greeks had become

orientalised, and the native inhabitants, the Copts, a small number of whom still exist, were merely their hewers of wood and drawers of water. Cæsar was a man of fifty-three when he met Cleopatra, and already the conqueror of the world. He had, says Anatole France, " exhausted all the glory and all the pleasures and had extracted from life all that it has to give in the way of violent emotions and excessive joys. His refined features had assumed the peaceful pallor of marble. It seemed that such a man would live henceforth only by and in his intellect. Yet he loved the Egyptian woman even to madness."

If Cleopatra had been born without beauty and without charm, neither Cæsar nor Mark Antony would have fallen in love with her and Cæsar might not have been assassinated, and Mark Antony might not have blundered to his ruin. Pascal's reflection is sufficiently familiar: " He who would thoroughly know the vanity of men has only to consider the causes and effects of love. The cause is a *je ne sais quoi*, an indefinable trifle—the effects are monstrous. If the nose of Cleopatra had been a little shorter, it would have changed the history of the world."

But would it ? Cæsar added mightily to his unpopularity by taking his Egyptian mistress to

2

Rome, but his course to dictatorship was set long before he met her, and it was the dictator and not the lover whom Brutus stabbed. And it is probable that the hot-headed Antony would have been destroyed by the crafty, calculating Octavius had he never met Cleopatra at Tarsus. In any case, if there had been no Cleopatra for Antony, there would have been another woman. He was the insatiable amorist.

" The cause is an indefinable trifle," says Pascal. " The effects are monstrous." But the moralist often exaggerates, and there is no subject on which there has been such persistent and fantastic exaggeration as the effect of sexual passion on human affairs. Who are the men and women who have bartered everything for a mad love affair ? Mary Stuart certainly, Charles Stewart Parnell perhaps. But who are the others among those who have had much to barter. I doubt, too, whether the little man or the little woman often buys love at a heavy price. The truth is that, despite the romanticists, love is for most men, and for most women perhaps, a soothing addition to life, perhaps an inspiration, perhaps an amusement, and perhaps escape, as I think it was to Nelson. There are some men for whom love is life. But they are generally poets or failures and, not infrequently, both.

Cleopatra was an amorist, but not an uncalculating amorist. Her lovers were the two greatest men of her time. It was possible, it must have seemed to her more than possible, that each in turn could assure her heart's desire. She was as ambitious as she was capable. If Cæsar had lived, he would probably have married her and she would have shared the Imperial throne. If Antony had won the battle of Actium, with him she would have ruled the Eastern world, secure on her throne in Alexandria. She lost. The luck was against her. But there was calculation in her playing of the game.

Cleopatra went with Cæsar to Rome, where, in the last years of his greatness, she lived in a villa, the gardens of which ran along the banks of the Tiber. Her life was secluded and discreet. She discussed literature and antiquities with Cicero as they walked under the pines. She received such men as Atticus, himself half a Greek with his complete Greek culture, the wealthy Lepidus and others of Cæsar's friends, for the time apparently indifferent to politics and to her claims as a queen, apparently entirely concerned with her lover and the son that she had borne him.

After Cæsar's assassination, Cleopatra realised that Rome would be no longer a safe place for her, and that the ambitions founded on her lover's eminence had been destroyed, and she hastily returned to Alexandria. For the next few years she had a short spell of peace and prosperity. She added to the beauty of her city with many magnificent buildings. She suppressed palace plots and intrigues. She showed herself the most capable of sovereigns. Cleopatra has frequently been accused of being the mistress of many lovers, Herod, King of the Jews, among the number. But there is absolutely no evidence of the truth of any of the stories except those that concern Cæsar and Anthony.

Civil war within the Roman Empire followed Cæsar's assassination. Mark Antony was elected Consul, but he was soon compelled to fight for his position against Octavius, Cæsar's nephew. After some inconclusive fighting, peace was patched up between them, and a new Triumvirate—Antony, Octavius and Lepidus—was established. But while the Triumvirs were busy pillaging Rome, each intent on adding to his own personal possessions, the East was still held by Brutus and Cassius, the two most notable of Cæsar's assassins. Both they and the Triumvirs begged Cleopatra for the loan of money and the supply of provisions. She was rich and an ally worth securing.

After some hesitation—for she never acted in a hurry—Cleopatra decided to side with the Triumvirs. She had known Antony in Rome. He was Cæsar's friend. After Cæsar's death, he had defended her in the Senate. A treaty was signed in which Rome recognised Cæsarion, Cæsar's and Cleopatra's son, as King of Egypt, and Cleopatra pledged herself to provision the Roman army being sent into Macedonia and to support the Roman forces with her fleet. The result of a brief campaign was Antony's complete victory at Philippi and the death of Brutus and Cassius. The victory made Antony master of the eastern half of the Roman Empire, and he was content that Octavius should preen himself in Rome while he made magnificent progresses through Greece and Asia Minor. Wherever he stayed his house was, says Plutarch, " the resort of obsequious kings and queens contending for his favour by their beauty and munificence." Antony was one of the many Romans of his day bitten by the East. He was fascinated by luxury and ostentation. Moreover, he was both a tumultuous and an histrionic man, always eager to live picturesquely.

He established his court at Tarsus in the year 42 B.C., preparing for a campaign against the Parthians, and from Tarsus he wrote letters to Cleopatra, urging her to visit him. But Cleopatra had no mind to become one more ornament in the conqueror's court. The practical division of the Roman Empire suited her own political ideas. Let the Empire be divided into two, then Egypt must be the centre of the eastern half and Alexandria its capital. But she must be Queen in Alexandria. She would go to Antony as an equal. Her visit must be granted as a favour. So she tarried and excused herself while Antony's impatience increased. And at last she arrived, sailing up the river Cydnus in her silver barge.

The French poet José Maria de Hérédia has written:

Sous l'azur triomphal, au soleil qui flamboie,
La trirème d'argent blanchit le fleuve noir,
Et son sillage y laisse un parfum d'encensoir,
Avec des chants de flute et des frissons de soie.

A la proue éclatante ou l'épervier s'éploie
Hors de son dais royal se penchant pour mieux voir,
Cléopâtre, debout dans la splendeur du soir,
Semble un grand oiseau d'or qui guette au loin sa proie.

Her entrance was admirably planned. She knew exactly how to catch her fish. She was seen, and conquered. From the moment that she landed at the quayside at Tarsus, Antony was hers. At first she was a little disappointed in him. When he had come to her garden by the Tiber, he had been carefully quiet and subdued. At Tarsus she found him boisterous and coarse in manner and speech. And Cleopatra was a fastidious Greek. But he was magnificently masculine and a conqueror, and Cleopatra could be all things to all men. She had little difficulty in persuading him to give up the projected expedition against the Parthians and to return with her to Egypt. The man of the camp found the super-luxurious life in Alexandria infinitely delightful. And imitating Cæsar before him, he loafed in Egypt while his wife, " the harsh and violent Fulvia," was fighting for him in Italy against Octavius.

In tempting him to remain with her, Cleopatra was as much politician as mistress. She dreamt of an Empire of the East. The first step towards it was to detach Antony from all interest in the West. She held him by suiting herself to his tastes. He loved dicing. She played dice with him. He loved hunting, and she, lazy and languorous though she was, hunted with him. She watched him, praising his strength and agility, while he was doing his military exercises, and of an evening she would dress as a boy and go with him into the streets of Alexandria, chaffing the people in the taverns and at the street corners, all of which he loved but which bored and irritated the Queen.

Call after call came to Antony from Italy, but he was deaf to them all. Rome could disappear in the Tiber for all he cared. But at last circumstances were too much for the lovers. Fulvia's forces were defeated and she was obliged to fly from Rome, and at the same time a great army of Parthians invaded the Roman province of Syria, which was Antony's particular possession. And reluctantly he sailed from Alexandria with a fleet of two hundred ships provided for him by the Queen. It is not to be forgotten that it added to Cleopatra's attraction that she was very rich, while the Roman always badly needed money.

Antony had become excessively popular in Alexandria. The people liked his rough humour. He was a friend of the Queen, but he was never offended by the most familiar jests made at his expense, and the crowd who watched him sail for Italy wished him a speedy return. Cleopatra was far too sure of herself to doubt that he would return, and perhaps she was not altogether sorry for a short respite from the taverns and the dicings and the rough embraces.

It was to be three years before she saw him again. Fulvia, an ambitious lady with a genius for quarrelling, had been largely responsible for her husband's break with Octavius Cæsar. She died before Antony reached Italy, and her death made a reconciliation between him and Octavius far easier. An agreement followed the reconciliation, exactly as Cleopatra desired and perhaps had dictated. The eastern part of the Empire went to Antony and the western to Octavius, and the new friendship was cemented, as Cleopatra certainly did not desire, by the marriage of Antony to Octavius's widowed sister, Octavia, an admirable lady of great beauty and considerable character.

Cleopatra was kept in close touch with what was happening in Rome, her principal agent being an Egyptian soothsayer whom Antony had taken with him from Alexandria, and who busied himself exciting in his master jealousy of Octavius and, when he dared, suggesting how inferior were the placid attractions of Octavia to the sensuous charm of Egypt's Queen. Public affairs compelled Antony to stay for some time at Athens, where Octavia bore him a daughter. Her influence was steadily for good, and in the three years that she was with Antony she prevented more than one quarrel between her husband and her brother.

In the year 37 B.C., Antony and Cleopatra met again. Octavia remained in Italy while her husband was settling affairs in Syria, and he once more sent for Cleopatra. She had not anticipated so

long a parting, and this time there was none of the
dalliance that she had shown four years before.
Immediately after her arrival she was rewarded
with the gift of provinces in Asia Minor and Syria,
including part of Judea, to add to her dominions.
But these new provinces had to be paid for at a
pretty high price from the well-filled Egyptian
treasury.

Antony certainly found Cleopatra a far more
amusing companion than the gentle Octavia, but
the resumption of their relations was again, and on
both sides, largely the result of political considerations. Antony always wanted money. Cleopatra was ceaselessly eager to add to the power and
prestige of her kingdom and herself without the
trouble and risk of conquest. The Egyptians were
never a warlike people. With their other relations, from the meeting in Syria until the end of
their lives, Antony and Cleopatra remained
mutually distrustful politicians, playing their own
hands, often treacherously.

As soon as the news reached Rome that Antony
and Cleopatra had met again, Octavia hurried east,
but at Athens she received letters from Antony
forbidding her to come any further. That was
Cleopatra's victory. But she was by no means
sure of Octavia's husband, and she used all the

wiles, that she knew so well, to keep him by her side. If he left her for a day she would burst into tears. She cut down her diet so that she might be supposed to be wasting away for love. She assured him that though she was a mighty queen, it was only for him that she cared, and that everything else might go. It suited Antony to pretend to be deceived. She was a delicious companion, anyhow, and he was a soldier, still in the prime of his manhood, hungry to rival the fame of Julius Cæsar, now dreaming of the conquest of Persia and badly needing Cleopatra's money for the equipment of his army.

At the beginning of the year 36 B.C., Antony and Cleopatra were married at Antioch, the Queen receiving the island of Cyprus and the land round Jericho as a wedding present. The Romans were monogamous, and this wedding, while Octavia was alive, was not only illegal for a Roman citizen, but an affront to Roman tradition. Cleopatra's plan had succeeded, and Mark Antony had come to regard himself as an Oriental king entitled to a harem of legitimate wives.

Almost immediately after the marriage, Antony started on the Persian expedition. It was a 1,200 miles march to the Persian frontier, and the journey took him five months. His army consisted of

100,000 men, the largest army ever commanded by
a Roman general. But in the early days of the
campaign he was weakened by treachery and
desertion. The summer operations brought him
no practical advantage, and, as winter came on, he
realised that retreat was inevitable. This retreat
across mountain passes, with continuous harassing
attacks from a mobile enemy, was the greatest
achievement of Antony's military career. He
held his forces together. He brought the Roman
Eagles back into Roman territory, but his losses
are said to have amounted to 20,000 men.

It has sometimes been suggested that his longing
to get back to Cleopatra had caused Antony to
abandon the Persian enterprise. The truth is,
that he had not the resources either in men or
material for carrying it on, and that the retreat was
dictated by sound military considerations. The unfortunate expedition, however, left Antony in a
very awkward position. The Romans were growing very tired of government by the Triumvirs, and
Rome never forgave failure. Even worse for
Antony, with his definitely Eastern ambitions, no
more money was to be had, for the time at least,
from Egypt. The Egyptians hated spending money
on armies. They infinitely preferred to pay
artists than to pay soldiers, and there were

always temples and palaces to be built and canals to be cut.

Cleopatra had opposed the Persian expedition and rejoiced at its failure. Now, she urged, Antony could be content to be King of Egypt and to join with her in developing the power of her kingdom. But Antony remained a Roman, and to him the title of Roman Proconsul was still greater than that of Egyptian King. He had inherited a tradition of conquest. It was pleasant to loaf at Alexandria, but it was the business of his life to fight, and Cleopatra had once again to employ all her ingenuity to keep him by her side. She urged that Italy was ruined by civil war, that Egypt was rich and might become richer, and that Antony could now establish an empire with Egypt as its centre and thus become a second Alexander. To please him, she organised one gorgeous festival after the other during the winter months, indulging in an orgy of grotesque wastefulness, once, so it is said, throwing a pearl worth some fifty thousand pounds to be dissolved in vinegar as a means of proving the extent of her resources. And once more she won.

Persia was forgotten, and in the spring of 34 B.C. Antony invaded Armenia, captured the King, married Alexander, the eldest of the sons that he had had by Cleopatra, to an Armenian princess, and returned to Alexandria with a vast quantity of plunder. The victory was celebrated with a splendid festival. Antony and Cleopatra, surrounded by their children, sat on two golden thrones erected on a silver platform. Cleopatra was proclaimed Queen of Kings. Julius Cæsar's son Cæsarion was proclaimed joint ruler with his mother, and to the other children the conquering Antony gave various provinces. But it was Cleopatra's triumph more than his.

It seemed that her political ambitions were fulfilled. The Eastern Empire was established, and now the Queen set out entirely to cut off Antony from Italy. She persuaded him to adopt Oriental dress. A temple was built in his honour, and he was worshipped as a god. But under the Oriental dress, and despite his abandonment of the toga, Rome and the Tiber were always in his mind. His life in Alexandria was a magnificent exile. He continued sending formal communications to the Senate as a Proconsul, and he steadily refused to divorce Octavia.

His hesitations did him little good. He was denounced in the Roman Senate. His children by Cleopatra were declared illegitimate, and Egypt was formally acclaimed a Roman province, and it became clear to Antony that his power could only be established by the conquest of Octavius. He gave up all thought of further Eastern conquest, and for the time was concerned only with directing intrigues in Rome, where there was a growing fear that Cleopatra was dreaming of setting up her own throne in the Capitol. "The Queen is preparing the world ruin of the Capitol and the funeral obsequies of the Empire."

As a matter of fact she was far too shrewd for any such dream, and was indeed already not a little fearful that the Romans would destroy what she had succeeded in establishing. She accordingly took immediate measures to equip a great fleet for defence and offence, and with it she sailed to meet Antony at Smyrna. He had been busy at Ephesus gathering a great army of mercenaries and had secured the more or less dependable assistance of a dozen of the petty kings of Asia Minor. At Ephesus, where Antony had his headquarters, Cleopatra arranged another series of banquets and processions in which soldiers and sailors from every corner of the earth had their part. Cleopatra was determined that, if she could not save her kingdom, its ruin should be "romantic and resounding." She would march with her army and live with her army, and the camp should have all the luxury of

a palace. She bought over the Romans on Antony's staff who were anxious to prevent a civil
war. She attended councils of war. She once
more tried to nag Antony into divorcing Octavia,
and to this he was finally persuaded. This was her
last triumph—and her ruin.

Antony was again denounced in the Senate, one
of the speakers asserting that Rome was becoming
the prize of a courtesan's favours, and war was
declared, not on Antony, but on Cleopatra.
Cleopatra was thoroughly afraid. The crews of her
fleet suffered severely during the winter. She had
a double anxiety. If Rome conquered, she would
lose her empire and her lover. She had a shrewd
suspicion of the power of her forces to face
Rome, and she was none too sure of Antony
altogether.

He was feeling the results of the debauchery of the last years. He had become feeble of
purpose. He could never make up his mind. His
strength was sapped.

The Roman and Egyptian fleets met at Actium
on September 2nd, 31 B.C. The fleets were each
over two hundred strong, and their relative qualities
were much those of the English and Spanish forces
in the battle of the Spanish Armada. Antony's
vessels were heavily armed, Octavius's light and

mobile. Fighting went on for some hours when Antony noticed that "the galley with the purple sails" which bore Cleopatra was sailing from the battle line. Then the lover overcame the soldier. Ambition was swamped by desire, and he followed her—I again quote Anatole France—"abandoning the battle by an astonishing act of cowardice which in such a soldier becomes heroic." The fight went on without him for some hours, but it ended with the destruction of his fleet, and Mark Antony sailed out of history on Cleopatra's galley with its purple sails, "sitting alone at the prow, his head in his hands."

In Alexandria, Antony had long consultations with Herod the King of Judea, and Herod advised him to make his peace with Rome by killing Cleopatra and once more bringing Egypt within the Roman orbit. But Antony remained faithful to his wife, and together they set about devising defence, building ships, recruiting soldiers, and pleasing the people with the usual prodigal festivities. But there was gloom in Alexandria, and the painted courtiers in the palace nicknamed themselves the Company of Death.

Deserted by his Roman staff officers, suspecting Cleopatra of intriguing with Octavius, weary and heartbroken, Antony was unable to protect Alexandria. Octavius entered the city on August 1st, 30 B.C. Antony committed suicide, and the conqueror allowed Cleopatra to bury him with all royal honours.

There is a story that Cleopatra set herself to the capture of Octavius as she had captured his uncle. Octavius was " a sickly, stammering, cowardly, cruel young man," patient, ambitious, suspicious, and in the end, as men with such qualities often are, entirely successful. Doubtless he in his turn was dazzled by the beautiful Greek. But it was not love or power that she wanted now, but rest and peace. She had loved Antony and her one desire was to die with him, while it was the will of Octavius that she should grace his triumphant return to Rome. But she secured exactly what she wanted, a gentle and easy imprisonment which she used to stage the death that she desired. An asp hidden in a basket of figs drove its poisoned fangs into her arm, and the Roman soldiers found the Queen lying dead on a golden couch. With her were her two faithful slaves, Charmion and Eiras, dying at her feet. " A good deed this, Charmion," said Eiras. " Yes, most goodly," was the reply, " and befitting the descendant of so many kings."

Horace has told the story of her death in one of his Odes:

With fearless hand she dared to grasp
The writhings of the wrathful asp,
And suck the poison through her veins,
Resolv'd on death, and fiercer from its pains:
Then scorning to be led the boast
Of mighty Cæsar's naval host,
And arm'd with more than mortal spleen,
Defrauds a triumph, and expires a queen.

Cleopatra died on August 31, 30 B.C., at the age of thirty-nine.

Octavius returned to Rome the first of the Roman Emperors. The children of Antony and Cleopatra were chained to his chariot as he made his entry into the Imperial City. A waxen image of the Queen was carried in the procession. Egypt was a Roman province. The glory of the city of Alexander the Great had departed. But in Alexandria the Queen was beloved and regretted. "She cannot therefore," says Anatole France, "have been as wicked as her enemies have declared. But we must not forget that beauty is one of the virtues of this world."

EDWARD III reigned in England from 1327 to 1377. As men count glory, these fifty years were glorious years. They were years of conquest, of the victories of Crécy and Poitiers, of the humiliation of Scotland. They were years of chivalry. They saw the institution of the Order of the Garter. Wycliffe, the first of the English religious reformers, and Chaucer, the Father of English Poetry, were born during Edward's reign. But with the glory there was tragedy—the Black Death with its unparalleled list of victims and the consequent revolution in England in the status of the day labourer. With the dawn of the fifteenth century, the sun of the Middle Ages had set.

The thirteenth century was the summer of the Middle Ages. "Everywhere," says Mr. Belloc, "Europe was renewed; there were new white walls around the cities, new white Gothic churches in the towns, new castles on the hills, law codified, the classics rediscovered, the questions of philosophy sprung to activity and producing in their first vigour, as it were, the summit of expository power in St. Thomas, surely the strongest, the most virile, intellect which our European blood has given to the world." The thirteenth century saw the greatest of the Plantagenets, Edward I, on the throne of England. In France it was the century of St. Louis.

The fourteenth century was—I quote Mr. Chesterton—"the April of patriotism, but the autumn of mediæval society." It was the century of Edward III of England and of the early and on the whole incompetent Valois kings of France. The English King claimed the French crown through his mother, Isabella, " the she-wolf of France," and the long struggle that he began, in mere vain personal ambition, lasted from 1346, the year of Crécy, until 1431, when, thanks to the military genius of Joan of Arc, England lost all its French possessions except the town of Calais.

The war, like all mediæval wars, was dynastic. The English people had no sort of interest in the conquest of French territory and in the destruction of French villages. But royal ambition and the military prowess of Edward III and his son, the Black Prince, incidentally played a considerable part in the history of the English people. The battle of Crécy and, to a less degree, the battle of

Poitiers were won by the skill of the English archers, mainly yeomen farmers tilling their own holdings, prosperous as the result of the admirable common-sense legislation of the Plantagenet kings, who fought against and defeated the chivalry of France. The history of Democracy might well begin with an account of the battle of Crécy.

These yeomen of England were doubtless resentful at being dragged from their holdings to fight the King's battles overseas, and, being English, they must certainly have been more than a little amused by the excessive courtesy of contending generals one to the other. On the night of the battle of Poitiers, so Froissart records:

" The prince made a supper in his lodging to the French king and to the most part of the great lords that were prisoners. And always the prince served before the king as humbly as he could, and would not sit at the king's board for any desire that the king could make; but he said he was not sufficient to sit at the table with so great a prince as the king was. Then he said to the king, ' Sir, for God's sake make no evil nor heavy cheer, though God this day did not consent to follow your will. For, sir, surely the king my father shall bear you as much honour and good will as he may do, and shall accord with you so reasonably that you shall ever be friends together after. And, sir, I think you ought to rejoice, though the day be not as you would have had it, for this day you have now the high renown of prowess, and have passed this day in valiantness all other of your party. Sir, I say this not to mock you, for all that be on our party, that saw every man's deeds, are plainly accorded by true sentence to give you the prize and chaplet.' Therewith the Frenchmen began to murmur, and said among themselves, how the prince had spoken nobly, and that by all estimation he should prove a noble man if God sent him life and to persevere in such good fortune."

While the English armies were fighting victoriously in France, the Black Death was decimating the English countryside. The plague first appeared in England in 1348. Its ravages lasted for nine years, with recurrences in 1361 and in 1368. Twenty-five million persons died in Europe, and in England the mortality was certainly half and possibly three-quarters of the total population. Mr. Belloc has said that " the great experiment of the Middle Ages could not recover from the devastation. The hymns of the ages of faith were lost in a twilight of death and desolation." In England the Law Courts were shut because the judges were dead. No masses were sung in many churches, for there were no priests to sing them.   The city streets were deserted; the fields of the countryside were untilled. Business was disorganised, food prices rose, famine threatened the land.   The Feudal System had been brought practically to an end by the development of Parliamentarianism in the reign of Edward III. It may be said to have died with the Black Death.

When the plague had run its course, labour was scarce and the labourer demanded so high a rate of wages that Parliament, in 1351, passed the Statute of Labourers, which established a legal rate of wages that forbade the landless man from moving from one county to another.   It was this legislation that was responsible for the Wat Tyler rebellion of the next reign.

King Edward III, himself, was a military commander of considerable talent, an energetic, good-tempered man, loving colour and pageantry, kindly, extravagant, and intensely self-indulgent.   Soldiering was his chief pursuit, but he was not without some element of statesmanship.   He encouraged Flemish weavers to stay in England—for generations it had been a wool-exporting country—and the beginning of a great national industry was due to his foresight.   Lucky in many things, in nothing was Edward III so lucky as in the lady who became his wife, Philippa of Hainault, one of the most gracious of English Queen Consorts, and included in these sketches as the type of the good wife.

In the year 1326, Isabella of France, consort of Edward II of England, journeyed from Paris to Cambrai, in these days a town on the Belgian-French frontier famous for its flax. Edward II was a crazy decadent, and, for some years, Isabella had carried on an intrigue with Roger Mortimer, one of the turbulent nobles of the Welsh Marches, who had gone with her to France, with the intention of raising forces to drive her husband from the English throne. With Isabella, who until she became a ferocious lunatic was a woman of outstanding charm, was her eldest son, afterwards Edward III, who was devoted to his mother and who for years refused to believe the stories of her scandalous doings. At Cambrai, the Queen and her son were received by Sir John of Hainault, brother of the Count of Hainault, a wealthy and important personage who kept his court at the adjacent town of Valenciennes, to which Isabella and Edward were escorted. The Count of Hainault had four daughters. It was with the second, Philippa, that the rather diffident, gauche English boy, not quite fourteen years old, fell in love. There is a contemporary description of Philippa when she was a child, hardly in her teens:

" The lady whom we saw has not uncomely hair, betwixt blue-black and brown. Her head is clean-shaped, her forehead high and broad, and standing somewhat forward. Her eyes are blackish brown and deep. Her nose is fairly smooth and even, save broad at the tip and also flattened, yet it is no snub nose. Her nostrils are also broad, her mouth fairly wide. Her lips rather full, especially the lower one. Her teeth which have fallen and grown again are white enough, the rest not so white. The lower teeth project a little beyond the upper, but this is little seen. Her eyes and chin are comely enough. Her neck, shoulders, and all her body and lower limbs are reasonably well shaped; and all her limbs well set and unmaimed, and nothing amiss so far as a man may see. Moreover she is brown of skin all over, and like her father, and in all things pleasant enough, as it seems to us. And the damsel will be of the age of nine years on St. John's day next to come, as her mother saith. She is neither too tall nor too short for her age, of fair carriage, and well taught in all that becometh her rank, and highly esteemed and well beloved of her father and mother, and of all her meinie in so far as we could learn the truth."

The Count of Hainault supplied Isabella with money and an army of two thousand, and it was agreed that, when once she had secured the throne of England for her son, he should marry Philippa. The Flemish mercenaries were commanded by Sir John of Hainault, and with Mortimer they landed at Harwich on September 25th. The King was intensely unpopular, and the Queen was generally beloved. She was received with enthusiasm in London, and Edward, lacking the pluck to put up any sort of defence, was arrested and imprisoned in Kenilworth Castle, where in 1327 he was compelled to sign an act of abdication. Edward III was crowned King in Westminster Abbey on February 1st. A Regency Commission was appointed, nominally to rule in his name, but actually the power remained with Isabella and her favourite. In the following March a special embassy was dispatched to Valenciennes formally to demand Philippa's hand in accordance with the arrangement made in the preceding autumn. Froissart relates:

" When they had shown the contents of their message, the earl said, ' Sirs, I thank greatly the king, your prince, and the queen his mother, and all other lords of England, since they have sent such sufficient personages as ye be to do me such honour as to treat for the marriage, to the which request I am well agreed, if our holy father, the pope, will consent thereto '; with the which answer

these ambassadors were right well content. Then
they sent two knights and two clerks immediately
to the pope to Avignon, to obtain a dispensation
for this marriage; for without the pope's license they
might not marry, for in the lineage of France they
were so near of kin as at the third degree, for the
two mothers were cousins german, issued of two
brethren. And when these ambassadors were
come to the pope, and their requests and considerations well heard, our holy father the pope, with all
the whole college, consented to this marriage, and
so feasted them. And then they departed and
came again to Valenciennes with their bulls. Then
this marriage was concluded and affirmed on both
parties . . . there this princess was married, by a
sufficient procuration brought from the king of
England; and after all feasts and triumphs done,
then this young queen entered into the sea at
Wysant, and arrived with all her company at
Dover. And sir John of Hainault, lord Beau-
mont, her uncle, did conduct her to the city of
London where there was made great feast. . . .
The English chronicle saith the marriage and coronation of the queen was done at York, with much
honour, the Sunday in the even of the conversion
of St. Paul, in the year of our Lord 1327 (N.S.
1328)."

A few weeks before the wedding, the boy King's father was brutally murdered in Berkeley Castle. His son was told that he had died a natural death, and he believed what he was told.

Philippa's beauty and her frank, gentle manners at once captured the heart of England, and it is characteristic of her that the first mention of her name in public documents is a record of her successful plea for pardon for a girl, under eleven years of age, convicted of robbery at York.

Philippa's first child, afterwards famous as Edward the Black Prince, was born at Woodstock, the house that she loved above all other places, on June 15th, 1530, much to the joy of England, for the young King and Queen had become national idols. Edward was now eighteen, and he was no longer ignorant of his mother's relations with Mortimer, nor could he longer tolerate their abuse of authority which was properly his. After considerable and reasonable hesitation, having made up his mind to act, he acted promptly. Mortimer was arrested in Nottingham, hurried to the Tower of London and hanged at Tyburn. Isabella, rendered raving mad by Mortimer's death, was taken to Castle Rising in Norfolk, where she lived for twenty-eight years. After a while she partially recovered her sanity and was permitted frequently

to be with the Court at Windsor. The kind-
hearted Philippa showed her fearsome mother-in-
law every possible consideration, and received an
autograph letter from the Pope commending her
kindness.

Philippa was a good wife in every sense of the
word. She bore her husband twelve children,
seven sons and five daughters. Two of the sons
died in infancy and three of the daughters died
unmarried, one of them during the Black Death.
The five sons who are remembered were Edward
the Black Prince, Lionel of Antwerp, Duke of
Clarence, Thomas of Woodstock, Duke of
Gloucester, and John of Gaunt and Edmund
of Langley the founders of the rival houses of
Lancaster and York. Incidentally Philippa's
money was of considerable use to her husband,
who frequently found it difficult to persuade
Parliament to pay for his expensive wars. For
his sake, she frequently pawned her jewels, and
besides financing wars she made a valuable con-
tribution to English learning by providing the
foundation of Queen's College, Oxford. Philippa,
indeed, was a learned lady, well educated for her
age and the patron both of Froissart and of
Chaucer.

In the year 1346, while Edward was besieging

Calais, King David of Scotland, the ally of the King of France, crossed the English border with an army of forty thousand men. Philippa at once hurried north and joined the English army at Auckland Castle. She was no Joan of Arc, however, and she was content, says the chronicler Holinshed, " to ride from rank to rank encouraging her people in the best manner she could, and, that done, she departed committing them and their cause to God the giver of all victories." The Queen said her prayers in Durham Cathedral while the army fought, the English archers winning one more victory for the English King.

After holding out for nearly a year, the burghers of Calais, whose splendid stubbornness remains a jewel in the story of France, were forced by starvation to surrender. In his Life of Queen Philippa, Mr. B. C. Hardy quotes the following contemporary poem:

" Oure horses, that were faire and fat,
　Are eaten up ilk one bidene;
　Have we neither coney nor cat,
　That they are not eaten, and houndes kene,
　All are eaten up full clene;
　Is neither living biche nor whelp,
　That is well in our semblance sene;
　And thai are fled that should us help."

Philippa had joined the King, and she was with him when he received the six burghers who had been selected to make submission, and whom, he ordered, should be immediately beheaded. I again turn to Froissart:

' Then the queen, being great with child, kneeled down and sore weeping said, 'Ah! gentle sir, since I passed the sea in great peril I have desired nothing of you, therefore I now humbly pray you, in honour of the Son of the Virgin Mary and for the love of me, that you will take mercy of these six burgesses.' The king beheld the queen, and stood still in thought a space, and then said, ' Ah, dame, I would you had been now in some other place; you make such request of me that I cannot deny you. Wherefore I give them to you to do your pleasure with them.' Then the queen caused them to be brought into her chamber, and made the halters to be taken from their necks, and caused them to be new-clothed, and gave them their dinner at their leisure. And then she gave each of them six nobles, and made them to be brought out of the host in safeguard and set at liberty."

England was happy and prosperous in this year 1347, little guessing that within twelve months it was to be scourged by the Black Death. Mediæval kings, however, were not easily turned from the pursuit of glory by plague, pestilence, or

famine, and it was at the height of the Black
Death that King Edward instituted the Order
of the Garter. There is no sort of truth in the
story that the Order took its name from the
Countess of Salisbury dropping her garter at a
Court ball. The garter was an established badge
of chivalry. The King was the sovereign of the
Order, and there were at the beginning twenty-
four Companions with the same number of
Dames de la Fraternité, of whom the Queen
was the first.

It seems probable that Philippa's frugal mind
revolted at the extravagance of jousts and tourna-
ments at a time of national sorrow. She was a
good mother and a careful housewife, those of her
accounts that are still preserved showing the possession of a most orderly mind, and she was to
have a share in the universal mourning, her
daughter Joan dying in Bordeaux of the plague
in 1348.

After the plague had subsided, Edward's main
interest was the enlarging and rebuilding of his
castle at Windsor, a work directed by William
of Wykeham, recently appointed Royal Surveyor,
who, largely owing to the friendship of Philippa,
was to become Bishop of Winchester and Chancellor
of England. It was during these happy days at

Windsor that news came of the Black Prince's victory at Poitiers and of his capture of King John of France. Edward, with his wife by his side, received his victorious son and his royal prisoner with full state ceremonial in Westminster Hall, afterwards, in the quaint manner of the times, giving a state banquet in honour of the French King. But John, not unnaturally, was silent and gloomy. When bidden to be merry, he replied, " How shall we sing the songs of the Lord in a strange land ?"

The story of Queen Philippa's days is one long record of practical and unostentatious good deeds. Her sister-in-law, Queen Joan of Scotland, found life intolerable with her husband and came south to live for five years in seclusion. Philippa constantly visited her, lent her money and nursed her in her last illness. The wife of her nephew William of Hainault, who suddenly lost his reason, came to England, where she too found a kindly refuge.

In 1361, the Black Prince married his father's cousin, Joan, Countess of Kent, generally known as the " Fair Maid of Kent," a lady years his senior, a widow, and the mother of four children. The Black Prince, a famous commander in his youth, could have married any princess in Europe, but, much against his father's will, he insisted on Joan, whose good looks were passing and whose temper was not of the best. Philippa, however, was present at the wedding and was unfailingly kind to her daughter-in-law.

It was about this time that Geoffrey Chaucer joined the household of Prince Lionel, Philippa's second son, and in 1360 Jean Froissart came from his home in Flanders with a letter of introduction to the Queen of England, bringing with him an account that he had written of the battle of Poitiers. He was received most graciously by Philippa, whom he described as " a very fair lady, sweet tongued and feminine, the most gracious queen, most liberal and most courteous that reigned in all her time." He was appointed one of her clerks, remaining in the royal service for five years, during which time he wrote the greater part of his Chronicles.

In 1366, Philippa's favourite son, Lionel, left England to marry the well-dowered daughter of De Visconti, Lord of Pavia. Lionel was a boastful, extravagant, ostentatious man of the smallest capacity, a widower with one daughter. He made a gorgeous progress through Europe with both Froissart and Chaucer in his suite. Stow wrote the following account of the wedding banquet in Milan:

"There were in one only course seventy goodly horses adorned with silk and silver furniture; and in another, silver vessels, falcons, hounds, armour for horses, costly coats of mail, breastplates glistering of massy steel, helmets and corselets decked with costly crests, apparelled distinct with costly jewels, soldiers' girdles, and lastly, certain gems by curious art set in gold and purple, and cloth of gold for men's apparel in great abundance. And such was the sumptuousness of that banquet that the meats which were brought from table would sufficiently have served ten thousand men."

The festivities lasted five months, and then Lionel died, as well he might, the chronicler noting that he had "addicted himself overmuch to untimely banquetings."

Philippa had one more year to live, and it was a very sad year. She grieved sorely for the death of Lionel. Her eldest son, the Black Prince, was fighting in France, mortally ill, not too happy, perhaps owing to his illness, indulging in feats of unbridled savagery. And the King had made life hard for her by installing in her household, a not uncommon habit of the times, a handsome vulgar strumpet, Alice Perrins, whom he loaded with presents. In the summer of 1369, two others of her sons, the Duke of Lancaster and Edmund of York, said good-bye to their mother for the last time and joined the army in France.

The Queen remained at Windsor during the summer with her youngest son, a boy of fourteen, her husband, and good William of Wykeham, with whom she discussed his plans for New College, Oxford, and a school at Winchester, and her own Queen's College in which she never lost interest. She died on August 15th. Froissart has described her last hours:

" When the good Lady perceived her end approaching, she called to the king, and extending her right hand from under the bedclothes, put it into the right hand of the king, who was very sorrowful at heart, and thus spoke: ' We have enjoyed our union in happiness, peace and prosperity; I entreat therefore of you that on our separation you will grant me three requests.' The king with sighs and tears replied, ' Lady, ask; whatever you request shall be granted.' ' My Lord, I beg you will acquit me of whatever engagements I may have entered into formerly with merchants for their wares, as well on this as on the other side of the sea. I beseech you also to fulfil what gifts or legacies I may have made or left to churches here or on the continent, where I have paid my devotions, as well as what I may have left to those of both sexes who have been in my service. Thirdly, I entreat that when it shall please God to call you hence, you will not choose any other sepulchre than mine, and will lie by my side in the cloister at Westminster.' The king in tears replied, 'Lady, I grant them.' Soon after, the good Lady made the sign of the cross on her breast, and having recommended to God the king and her youngest son Thomas, who was present, gave up her spirit, which I firmly believe was caught by the holy angels and carried to glory in heaven, for she had never done anything by thought or deed which could endanger her losing it."

Philippa was buried in Edward the Confessor's chapel in Westminster Abbey, and when he died her husband's body was buried by her side. The poet Skelton translated her Latin epitaph. The following are the last lines of the translation:

A fruitful mother Philippe was, full many a son she bred,
And brought forth many a worthy knight, hardy and full of
    dread ;
A careful nurse to students all, at Oxford she did found
Queen's College, and Dame Pallas school, that did her fame
    resound.

Her debts, as she had requested, were all paid, and her last wishes were generally faithfully carried out.

Philippa was dead, but Alice Perrins remained, the old King becoming more doting as time went on. The Black Prince died in 1376, followed by his father one year later, worn out and weary in mind and body. His career has been summarised by Froude: " Under him England was successful in battles but defeated in war." As for his wife, I can do no better than quote Mr. Hardy's tribute:

" The tenderest of mothers, the most devoted of wives, and never more royal than when she occupied herself about the smallest detail of her people's lives, she seems, indeed, as Froissart painted her, ' *la plus gentil roine, plus large et plus courtoise que oncques regna en son temps.*' "

There is a monument to Queen Philippa in every old-fashioned English garden. After her marriage, her mother sent her as a present the first plants of rosemary ever grown in this country, together with a manuscript describing the virtues of the plant. In this manuscript, preserved in the library of Trinity College, Cambridge, there is recorded, says Miss Rohde, an old tradition: " Rosemary passeth not commonly in height the height of Christ while He was a man on earth," and that when the plant attains the age of thirty-three years it will increase in breadth but not in height.

" There's rosemary, that's for remembrance " of, in Froissart's words, " that kind lady who in all honour without blame passed her life."

HUME has declared that St. Joan was " one of the most striking characters on the stage of history." Voltaire lampooned her as fantastically immoral, Sismondi pitied her as " the victim of fraudulent priests," Michelet endeavoured to explain away the miracles of her life by underestimating its achievement. To Jules Favre she is " the ideal democrat." Gabriel Hanotaux has said that she was " naturally supernatural," whatever that may mean. Anatole France deplored " the perpetual hallucination of her unbalanced mind." Andrew Lang paid admiring tribute to her as " the most perfect daughter of her Church." To Mark Twain the maid was, as Mr. Shaw has said, " an unimpeachable American schoolteacher in armour," and to Mr. Shaw himself she is " one of the first Protestant martyrs."

This variety of judgments suggests that the common answer to the question " What went ye out for to see ?" is " What we particularly wanted to see." Most historians write with a purpose.

They start with a moral that they wish to enforce and a conclusion that they wish to reach, and they colour and arrange the facts to suit their purpose. Voltaire, Michelet, Hanotaux and Anatole France are anti-clerical and materialist in various degrees. How can they admit that France was saved by the intervention of angels and saints? Mr. Shaw remains an Irish Protestant, a far tougher proposition than the American Protestant at whom he laughs in the person of Mark Twain, and for all his admiration, he cannot attach any " objective validity to the form of St. Joan's visions." The trouble is that, in colouring the facts to suit the individual taste and ignoring the facts when they do not fit preconceived theories, the historian is constantly landed in palpable absurdities. His hatred of the Catholic Church compelled Froude to become the apologist of Thomas Cromwell, demonstrably a mean and sorry rascal. In his endeavour to prove that Whiggery was sent down from Heaven, Macaulay was obliged (surely against his better judgment) to make a hero of Dutch William.

It has become the fashion to exaggerate the complexity of human nature. Most of us, the great as well as the humble, the highly placed as well as the obscure, are really very simple. Such phrases as " sex complex " and so on are the merest jargon invented to deceive and as meaningless as the assurance of the doctor of Victorian times that his patients needed "toning up."

The truth about St. Joan of Arc is of the simplest. She was a saint. Just that. The unparalleled service that she rendered to France in two short years could only have been possible for a girl guided, inspired and inflamed by miraculous forces which the scientist may try to explain away but which he can never explain.

A saint is a genius who realises that his exceptional powers are derived directly from God, who devotes himself, without hesitation or qualification, to the carrying out of what he knows is the divine purpose, who seeks no personal gain or glory, who puts aside all thought of personal gratification, who is the conscious servant of the Almighty, and nothing more nor less. Saints have often apparently failed. They have often died with a dreadful sense of humiliation and despair. Their guerdon, indeed, is never of this world. Consequently, it would seem certain that, in every generation, there have been saints whose saintliness has never been recognised. There are slum saints as well as village Hampdens. But this does not affect the truth that, now and again, a stupendous figure appears, a St. Francis, a St. Joan, a St. Teresa, for whom difficulty, opposition and misunderstanding have no sort of meaning and who achieve the impossible.

St. Joan's career is perfectly understandable if that shrewd young woman is believed, if it is accepted that she told the truth and that she was actually inspired and guided by St. Michael, St. Catherine, and St. Margaret. Her military triumphs are monstrously incredible if it is supposed that she was the victim of hysteria. Hallam says: " We cannot pretend to explain the surprising story of the Maid of Orleans; for, however easy it may be to suppose that a heated and enthusiastic imagination produced her own visions, it is a much greater problem to account for the credit they obtained and for the success that attended them." St. Joan was, as a matter of fact, the very last type of young woman to be the victim of hysterical hallucination. She was, Mr. Shaw says, " a sane and shrewd country girl of extraordinary strength of mind and hardihood of body." Her contemporaries record that she was tall and good-looking and well-proportioned. " Her features were feminine if somewhat rustic, but showed great intelligence, firmness and gentleness." Her face was oval and regular, and there was a look of deep earnestness in her thoughtful dark eyes. Her forehead was high, denoting mental power, her nose straight, her mouth small with thin red lips, her neck well formed, and her long hair fell over her strong shoulders. She was quick-witted, frank, simple, a true peasant of Lorraine with a love of nature that links her to St. Francis of Assisi, and a quickness of judgment that amazed the judges, intent on contriving her death. Hallucination is common enough among the over-civilised, the over-pampered and the over-fed. But hysteria has never been the disease of men and women who live an open-air life, who are sufficiently well fed—St. Joan's father was a comparatively well-to-do peasant proprietor—and who have acquired their knowledge of life in the village and the field.

It is said, again, that St. Joan's voices were the result of her excessive piety. Certainly she was a pious Catholic. Certainly, from the point of view of the modern Protestant and the modern agnostic, she may be regarded as superstitious, but no more than modern men like Von Hügel and Pasteur. In her examination she stoutly denied that she believed in fairy rings or the witches' Sabbath or any other of the familiar rural superstitions. Constancy in prayer is not really conclusive evidence of weakness of intellect. St. Teresa, one of the most practical and one of the most domineering women in history, prayed quite as fervently as St. Joan.

It would be comfortable for modern scepticism if the fact that St. Joan went regularly to church could be regarded as sufficient evidence that her Voices had no objective existence.   But can it ?

Further it is argued that the angels who advised her were familiar to her through long association in picture and in image. As a matter of fact, there was no statue of St. Michael in the village church at Domrémy, and it would seem probable that St. Joan had never heard either of St. Margaret or St. Catherine. The strange fact is—call it a coincidence if you will—that St. Catherine of Alexandria was put to death at the age of eighteen and that St. Margaret of Antioch suffered martyrdom when she was nineteèn.   It is curious, to put it at the lowest, that it was these two saints who were chosen to be the guides of a girl who was herself to die a horrid death in the Market Place at Rouen before she was twenty.   St. Michael, too, leader of the warriors of Heaven, was selected with dramatic appropriateness to spur on Joan to great and decisive military achievement.

The practical result of St. Joan's inspiration is outside the possibility of doubt, and this despite Anatole France's strained endeavour to minimise the military and political importance of raising the siege of Orleans and defeating the English at Patay.

"Her Voices," says Jules Quicherat, the free-thinking historian to whom the world is indebted for the details of St. Joan's life, "were far from entertaining her with idle dreams by which morbid imaginations deceive themselves." She was told that, on account of her virtues and her humility, she had been chosen to drive the English from the walls of Orleans and to secure the coronation of Charles the Dauphin in the Cathedral at Rheims. All that she was told she had to do she accomplished. She broke the power of the English, she secured their final evacuation of France, she made possible and indeed inevitable the gradual development of a united French nation.

She was promised for herself no sort of earthly reward, and indeed, from the beginning, she appears to have foreseen the fate that was awaiting her. "Did you know you were to be taken?" she was asked after her capture. "I thought it likely," she replied. "Then why, if you thought it likely, did you not take better care on the day you were captured?" "I knew neither the day nor the hour when I should be taken nor when it should happen." She was the girl with a mission, inspired by something, outside herself, making for victory.

The facts are clear. St. Joan declared that, for seven years, she was in constant communication with St. Michael, St. Catherine and St. Margaret, and that from them she received certain instructions, which she carried out with complete success. It has never been really suggested that she was a conscious liar, and the reality of the experiences which she declared were hers are confirmed by her qualities. She certainly was not morbid, and she certainly was practical. Her intelligence was above the average. As James Russell Lowell said: " The child, who, without any resources of her own, wrought such marvels, cannot reasonably be classed as a mental case."

She was not quite thirteen when she began to hear Voices. She was still a child when she understood the task with which she was to be entrusted. Because she was practical and shrewd, she was naturally terrified and disinclined to obey.

It is almost the truth to say that when St. Joan was born there were no Frenchmen in France. There were Armagnacs and Burgundians and English, but France, one and indivisible, had yet to be created. The English held the north and the west; the district between the Loire and the Somme was a desert. Villages were half destroyed. Many of the people were starving. Even in far-away Lorraine the effect of the constant fighting was bitterly realised by the people.

In 1415, three years after St. Joan's birth,
Henry V won the battle of Agincourt. Three
years later the English occupied Normandy, and
their allies, the Burgundians, controlled Paris.
In 1420, by the Treaty of Troyes, Henry V agreed
to marry Catherine of France, and on the death of
her father, Charles VI, he was to become King of
France as well as of England. The Dauphin,
afterwards Charles VII, known, thanks to Joan,
as " the Victorious," has been not unfairly drawn
by Mr. Shaw. Anatole France says of him:

"He was but a poor creature withal, the
eleventh of the miserable children born to the
mad Charles VI and his prolific Bavarian queen
He had grown up among disasters, and had sur-
vived his four elder brethren. But he himself was
badly bred, knock-kneed and bandy-legged; a
veritable king's son, if his looks only were considered, and yet it was impossible to swear to his
descent. Through his presence on the bridge at
Montereau on that day when, according to a wise
man, it were better to have died than to have
been there, he had grown pale and trembling,
looking dully at everything going to wrack and
ruin around him. After their victory of Verneuil
and their partial conquest of Maine, the English
had left him four years' respite. But his friends,

his defenders, his deliverers had alike been terrible. Pious and humble, well content with his plain wife, he led a sad, anxious life in his château on the Loire. He was timid. And well he might be so, for no sooner did he show friendship towards or confidence in one of the nobility than that noble was killed." Charles was poverty-stricken, a coward, "dwarfed in mind and body."

Orleans, which the Dauphin still contrived to hold, was the key of the south. The English were eager for its capture, because with Orleans in their hands the whole of France must be theirs, and it was in raising the siege of Orleans and in winning the subsequent battle at Patay, one of the definitely decisive battles of the world, that St. Joan saved France. And St. Michael, it will be remembered, was very clear about it. It was no vague commission that was given her. She was to go to Orleans, and Hume says: "The eyes of all Europe were turned towards this scene where it was reasonably supposed the French were to make their last stand for maintaining the independence of their monarchy and the rights of their sovereign." The Voices appear to have told St. Joan much of the history of her country, and St. Michael may have given her many suggestions that proved useful in her military career. Who knows?

As I have said, she hesitated, but she was assured that nothing was impossible to God, and at last, when, although she did not know it, any further hesitation would have been fatal, literally and figuratively she put on the armour of the Lord. Her father stormed at St. Joan when she made up her mind to be a soldier, just as St. Teresa's father stormed at her when she had made up her mind to be a nun.   But there were strong-willed women in the fifteenth and sixteenth centuries as there are strong-willed women in ours.   "As soon as I had consented," said St. Joan, "I felt that even if I had a hundred fathers and a hundred mothers who wished to restrain me, I should have gone."

St. Joan interviewed the trembling Dauphin at Chinon on March 26th, 1429.   She arrived at Orleans on April 29th.   The siege was raised on May 8th. St. Joan defeated the English at Patay on June 18th, and on July 17th Charles was crowned at Rheims.   The saint attacked Paris on September 8th, and on the following May 23rd she was cap-tured at Compiègne.   The deeds that have given her a unique place in history thus took place within a few weeks longer than a year.

St. Joan is the greatest amateur soldier in history, and if there was one thing made clear in the Great War it was that the amateur soldier is often the superior of the professional. The two qualities necessary for the winning of battles are courage and commonsense, and the reason why so many battles have been lost is that the professional soldier, while rarely lacking in courage, is as rarely endowed with any great measure of commonsense.

The first thing that St. Joan did was to persuade the French soldiers, who had been routed in so many battles, that they could beat the English if they chose, and to do this she imbued them with a new faith. They were no longer fighting for a king whom they probably did not know, and whom if they had known they would have despised. They were fighting for God and for their country, and by their country she meant the villages where they were born, the women whom they loved, and the children who called them father. The soldiers became crusaders, singing the *Veni Creator* as they were led to battle by the saint in armour. But the saint in armour remained as shrewd as the peasant girl tending her sheep. Michelet pays tribute to her "unfailing good sense." She was prompt in decision, she insisted on discipline, she would not tolerate foul language in the ranks. She was indeed, as Mr. Shaw has called her, "a born boss." So indeed was St. Teresa. So indeed have been most of the saints. The children of light have sometimes been far more than a match for the children of this world.

Soldiers have often been the victims of grotesque theories. St. Joan was a commonsense general, Her tactics were—I quote Andrew Lang—" to concentrate quickly, to strike swiftly, to strike hard, to strike at vital points, and, despising vain, noisy skirmishes and valiances, to fight with invincible tenacity of purpose." When the English were beaten their generals of course explained that they were beaten by witchcraft. As a matter of fact, they were beaten by commonsense, but commonsense always appears witchcraft to the military mind. As a military commander St. Joan had the swiftness of a Napoleon and the calmness of a Joffre. She always hated killing, but when it was necessary for victory, she could be quite ruthless. She fought for a purpose, for what to her was a divine purpose, and not being a fool, when she fought, she fought with the gloves off.

St. Joan first created an army and then she created a nation. When she first rode into the Dauphin's camp she found an undisciplined rabble into whom she literally put the fear of God and made them a victorious army, and a few weeks later, first on the field of Patay and second in the Cathedral at Rheims, she created a nation.

Mr. Shaw has attempted to picture St. Joan as the first of the Protestants. The truth is that she was one of the first of the nationalists. She laid the foundation stone on which Henry of Navarre, Richelieu, Louis XIV and the Revolutionists were to build. She inflamed national pride, she made great lords and peasants realise that it was a fine thing to be a Frenchman and that, being born French, they had better see to it that they were decent French. The Chanoine Rousseil quotes a jingle of the times:

> Sous l'estendart de la Poucelle
> Un de nous vaut mieux que cent.

The progresses that she had decided or which were decided for her had the greatest possible dramatic value—first Orleans and half France saved from the alien invaders, then Rheims with France once more with a crowned king of its own, and finally Paris, the recovery of the capital. Paris was never recovered by St. Joan, but it became French five years after her martyrdom.

Anatole France professes to regard the coronation in Rheims Cathedral as a mere showy waste of time. As a matter of fact, in its mystic symbolism, it had as great an influence on the French mind as the saving of Orleans. It is one of the inevitable deficiencies of the sceptic never to be able to realise the practical value of Catholic symbolism, and it should be remembered that the coronation of a Catholic king is as much a service of the Church as the Mass itself. St. Joan's achievement was very fairly summarised by the English chronicler Holinshed, who, writing one hundred and fifty years after her death, said:

" A young wench of an eighteene years old; of favour was she counted likesome, of person stronglie made and manlie, of courage great, hardie, and stout withal, and understander of counsels though she were not at them, she had great semblance of chastitie both of body and behaviour, the name of Jesus in her mouth at all her businesses, humble, obedient, and fasting divers days in the week. A person (as their books make her) raised up by power divine, onlie for succour to the French estate, then deeplie in distress."

The capture, the prolonged trials, the torture and finally the burning of the Maid present a series of problems to be understood only if they are approached with something of the Maid's own commonsense, with no attempt to whitewash personalities or institutions or to twist facts. It is quite true, as Mr. Shaw insists, that St. Joan was tried as a heretic and a sorceress, as an offender, that is to say, against the Church of whom she was the simple devoted child. But though St. Joan was tried by an ecclesiastical court for an ecclesiastical offence, she was actually tortured and burned because she had proved herself a dangerous enemy to the Anglo-Burgundian domination of France. The court that tried her was constituted strictly according to precedent and canon law, but the judges, and particularly the presiding judge, were creatures of the English. Mr. Shaw has attempted a bold whitewashing of Pierre Cauchon, the Bishop of Beauvais. He is made to say, when he returns to earth in the epilogue of Mr. Shaw's play:

" They will be the worse for remembering me: they will see in me evil triumphing over good, falsehood over truth, cruelty over mercy, hell over heaven. Their courage will rise as they think of you, only to faint as they think of me. Yet God is my witness I was just: I was merciful: I was faithful to my light: I could do no other than I did."

Pierre Cauchon was neither merciful nor was he faithful to any sort of light. He has been described as " a great and pompous clerk of the University of Paris," and the masters and doctors of the University of Paris were pro-English to a man. Anatole France says:

" They were Burgundians and English by neces-

sity and by inclination; they observed faithfully
the Treaty of Troyes, to which they had sworn;
they were devoted to the Regent, who showed them
great consideration; they abhorred the Armagnacs, who desolated and laid waste their city, the
most beautiful in the world; they held that the
Dauphin Charles had forfeited his rights to the
Kingdom of the Lilies. Wherefore they inclined
to believe that the Maid of the Armagnacs, the
woman knight of the Dauphin Charles, was inspired by a company of loathsome demons. These
scholars of the University were human; they believed what it was to their interest to believe; they
were priests, and they beheld the Devil everywhere,
but especially in a woman. Without having devoted themselves to any profound examination of
the deeds and sayings of this damsel, they knew
enough to cause them to demand an immediate
inquiry. She called herself the emissary of God,
the daughter of God; and she appeared loquacious,
vain, crafty, gorgeous in her attire. She had
threatened the English that if they did not quit
France she would have them all slain. She commanded armies, wherefore she was a slayer of her
fellow-creatures and foolhardy. She was seditious,
for are not all those seditious who support the
opposite party ?"

While she was still triumphant, St. Joan had already been found guilty by the Paris doctors of offences against God because of her offence against the masters of the men who were to be her judges. There was a long-sighted policy in the consent of the English Council to permit St. Joan to be tried by an ecclesiastical court, which, if it solemnly declared that the woman who had conducted the Dauphin to Rheims was a witch, would, it was suggested, utterly discredit the French cause. " The trial of the Maid would be the trial of Charles VII, the condemnation of the Maid the condemnation of Charles VII."

The Maid was taken from Compiègne to Beaulieu and from Beaulieu to Cambrai, where she was treated with singular kindness by two great ladies, and where, against the advice of her Voices, she attempted to escape. From Cambrai St. Joan was taken to Arras and then to Dieppe, and so on to Rouen, where she was locked in a tiny cell with shackles on her feet and a chain round her waist, with English soldiers day and night in her prison.

The jury of learned men summoned to assist St. Joan's two judges, the Bishop and the Inquisitor, was carefully packed. No bishop or doctor was summoned who should be suspected of the slightest sympathy with French nationalism.

St. Joan, left without counsel to help her, defended herself both with sagacity and courage. She realised that the jury was packed, and she demanded that a number of bishops with French sympathies should be summoned to attend, a request that was of course refused. The trial was indeed not a trial, but a battle. " From the very outset," says Anatole France, " these theologians and this damsel regarded each other with mutual horror and hatred." On the one side were venal theologians " inflated with knowledge and stuffed with scholasticism," on the other—and this is a very fine phrase of Anatole France's—" the fair inspired, frank of mind, capricious and enthusiastic."

The records of the trial have been carefully preserved, and to read them is to be charmed by the girl's amazing qualities. There is the little touch of modest boastfulness in " for spinning and sewing I am as good as any woman in Rouen," and the fine confession of a noble faith in her statement that the voice of the angel " taught me to live well, to go to church, and it told me to fare forth into France."

The judges were obdurate. With infinite patience they dug pitfalls for her feet, eager to find justification for the crime on which they had already decided. Within the public galleries there

was quite another feeling. " By my troth, she is a
good woman," said one English nobleman. " Why
is she not English ?"

The Church was suffering from the Great Schism
when St. Joan took her trial. There was Pope and
anti-Pope, and such questions were put to the girl
as " Whom think you to be the true Pope ?" in
order that her ignorance might betray her.

She was found guilty, of course. She was
preached at and insulted, her King being openly
denounced as a heretic and a schismatic. She
appealed to the Pope, and the appeal was never
submitted. She was threatened with torture, and
at last and for a time her spirit was broken, and she
professed willingness to submit to her judges.
Then there was trouble. The English suspected
treachery. The woman was a witch; how else
could she have beaten the English soldiers ? Let
the witch be burned without any more cackle.
That was the English way. But the recantation
was accepted, and St. Joan was ordered to perpetual
imprisonment, the Duchess of Bedford, knowing the
purity both of her body and mind, doing something
to protect her from the brutality of the English
soldiery. But St. Joan's mood of terrified submission did not last long. Back in her man's
clothes, she again played the man. The English

had their way, the Bishop of Beauvais being by no means unwilling, and St. Joan was burned alive in the Market Place of Rouen, repeating the name of " Jesus " six times before she died. Her heart and entrails were found intact when the fire had burnt out, and they were thrown into the Seine.

The Chanoine Rousseil endeavours to defend the Church in France from the guilt of St. Joan's martyrdom, and it is certainly true, as Leo XII said, that " those who condemned Joan of Arc were the worst enemies of the Holy See." The Chanoine Rousseil asserts that the Bishop of Beauvais and the doctors of Paris suffered badly from Gallicanism, that they were unfaithful to the Papal principle, that they were nationalists, and so on. There is a suggestion of truth in this. It is also true that the great majority of the secular clergy and possibly of the bishops in France knew that St. Joan was guiltless. It is true that the Franciscans were her friends as the Dominicans were her enemies. But it is also true that no voice of ecclesiastical authority was raised to save her life. The Church was as dumb as the King whom she had made, and there is more than a little force in Anatole France's gibe at priests and bishops: " If what they had once believed they still held to be true, if they believed that the Maid had come from

God to lead their king to his glorious coronation, then what are we to think of those clerks, those ecclesiastics who denied the Daughter of God on the eve of her passion ?"

St. Joan died in 1431. In 1436 Charles VII re-entered Paris. In 1455 Pope Calixtus III appointed a Commission to reconsider the charges made against the Maid. A large number of witnesses were examined, though in the twenty-four years that had passed many of those who knew the most of St. Joan and her achievements had died. The Commission was rather half-hearted. It was declared that St. Joan was "simple save in deeds of war, wherein she was well skilled." But the sentence of 1431 was nullified and pronounced invalid. But St. Joan was dead and for a time apparently forgotten by the France which she had served so well. François Villon, the poet-thief, remembered her, Montaigne made pilgrimage to her house at Domrémy; but there is hardly a mention of her in the literature of the centuries that followed until Voltaire wrote of her with luscious obscenity, and it was not until the dawn of the nineteenth century and the coming of Chateaubriand that St. Joan of Arc found her true place in the history of France, and it was not until 1920 that she was formally numbered with the saints.

The greatest mystery remains. Here was a young girl quite obviously, as it seems to me, divinely inspired for a gigantic task. As the Pope Benedict XV said: " We can only fully understand her in the light of Heaven." Why was she suddenly abandoned ? Why did the Voice that led her to victory lead her to death ? I know no answer to these questions. It is certainly true that death, and often cruel death, has been the lot of the most conspicuous servants of God and His Church. We others can only wonder. But it may be suggested that it was her horrible death that has given St. Joan her immortality here on earth and that has made her the most attractive of national saints. It is good that one should perish that the nation may live.

ST. TERESA

THE Moors invaded Spain at the beginning of
the eighth century, and the victory of Gua-
dalete in the year 711 made them masters of the
peninsula. It remained in their power until the
fall of Granada, nearly eight hundred years later,
and it was only the victory of Charles Martel, at
the battle of Tours in 733, that prevented a complete domination of Western Europe by the Moors,
whose armies had crossed the Pyrenees. That
mountain range was to be the limit of Moslem
European conquest. A few years later, Charle-
magne, filled with Christian enthusiasm, attempted
the subjugation of the Moslem power in Spain, but
his expedition ended in disaster.

The history of the Moorish occupation of Spain
is one of the curiosities in the story of civilisation
and culture. The Moslems' sweep westward absolutely destroyed the Roman and primitive Christian
civilisation on the south shore of the Mediterranean.
It is difficult in these days to remember that
St. Augustine, the greatest of the Doctors of the

Church, was the Bishop of Hippo, near Carthage. But it was the Arab scholars and, as I am convinced, much more the Jewish scholars whom they protected, who were the guardians of the Greek learning, which was lost to Europe during the Dark Ages. All that was best in Moslemism, its humanism and its scholarship, flourished for centuries in Spain and particularly in the kingdom of Andalusia and in the city of Cordova.

It was a beautiful city filled with noble buildings, adorned with wondrous bridges, notably clean, and though the great Jewish Aristotelian scholar Maimonides, who was born at Cordova, spent his life in Egypt, his family escaping from the Spanish city in one of the sporadic outbursts of Moslem persecution, it was at the University of Cordova that Aristotelian philosophy was preserved, while it was utterly unknown in Europe generally. There is a legend that it was from a Moslem, or probably from a Jewish, doctor from Cordova that St. Thomas Aquinas learned to write Greek and also learned the principles of Aristotle which, thanks to his scholarship, fundamentally changed the philosophy of the Catholic Church.

The renaissance of Christian nationalism in Spain began in the middle of the fifteenth century. Granada was captured from the Moors in the year

1491, twelve years after a national monarchy had been established by the marriage of Ferdinand of Arragon with Isabella of Castile. Eleven years previously, the Inquisition had been established in Castile to become within a very few years, not only the hammer of the Church but—a fact that is often forgotten—a popular national institution, and with the rise of a triumphant nationalism came the perfectly natural revolt against the presence in the country of capable and wealthy aliens.

The Jews were expelled in 1492, and during the last years of the fifteenth century the Inquisition, under the direction of Torquemada, carried on a relentless war against Jews and Saracens. Economically and intellectually, the expulsion of the Jews and of the Moors, which followed some years later, was an incalculable loss to Spain, but it is to be remembered that the loss occurred at the time of national rebirth, and in the glories of the joint reign which saw the discoveries of Columbus and the foundation of the Spanish Empire on the American continent.

In the year 1516, Ferdinand died and was succeeded by his grandson, Charles of Hapsburg, afterwards the Emperor Charles V. Under the rule of the Hapsburgs—Charles V himself was rarely in the country—and particularly during the reign of his son Philip, the husband of Queen Mary of England, Spain became the spear-point in the fight against the new heresies. It was in this new Spain, rescued from the cultured Moslem by the fundamentalist Catholic, that St. Teresa was born in the year 1515.

The sixteenth century was the century of achievement, the age of the great adventurers and the great artists, of a reawakened Europe broken in two in its awakening, of great ambitions and many wars, of the Renaissance and the Reformation and—a fact generally forgotten in England—of the Counter-Reformation. The story of the Counter-Reformation, with its reforming Popes, its stern suppression of ecclesiastical abuses, its recovery of the allegiance of Southern Europe, its enthusiasm for social service, shown in the careers of such men as St. Philip Neri and St. Vincent de Paul, has never been adequately written in a popular English form. Nothing could be better calculated to dispel illusions and to give a true idea of the nature of the Catholic Church.

Spain was unaffected by the teaching of the Reformers. She remained the faithful child of the Church. And in Spain the age of the Counter-Reformation saw the careers of two of the most inspired of modern mystics, St. Teresa and St. John of the Cross.

It is natural and inevitable that to average Englishmen the sixteenth century is the age when God's Englishmen, Frobisher and Drake, Grenville and Raleigh and the rest, bashed away success- fully and heroically against the devils of Spain. I imagine that few books have led to so great a misconception of the past as Charles Kingsley's *Westward Ho!*—the mischief it has wrought being due to the magnificently dramatic swing of the narration. To Kingsley, every Elizabethan was a hero, every Spaniard a priest-ridden craven, every English Roman Catholic a traitor, and every Jesuit a heartless liar. The truth is less flattering to English national pride. It is not necessary to attempt to palliate or defend the activities of the Inquisition either in Spain or in America, though the Inquisition was certainly not an unpopular institution in Spain. It is not to be denied that the chivalry of Spain, excited perhaps to an absurd extent by the expulsion of the Moors from the peninsula, regarded the extirpation of heresy as its first duty. But it is necessary to insist that the chivalry of Spain was a very real and a very splendid thing, finding its finest expression in the person of Don John of Austria, half-brother of

Philip II, who, thirteen years after Elizabeth ascended the English throne, broke the power of the Turks, the enemies of the faith, at the battle of Lepanto. There is no more attractive and appealing fighting man in European history, and if he had married Mary, Queen Elizabeth's cousin, as it was proposed, he might well have materially altered the history of the Church and of the Continent.

It was the habit of the well-born youth of sixteenth-century Spain to go, as a matter of course, to the Americas—four of St. Teresa's brothers were among the emigrants—not merely in search of fortune, like the English merchant adventurers, but to extend the dominion of the King and of the Cross. The Spanish soldier, simple as well as gentle, was a first-class fighting man, as was proved on the battlefields of Flanders. It may have been a good thing that the might of Spain was broken. But it is as stupid as it is mean to fail to appreciate the fine qualities of the men who gave their lives for a dying cause. As for the Church itself, there is no greater chapter in the record of missionary adventure than that of the Jesuits in South America. They were the protectors of the natives, the friends of the oppressed, showing the same combination of sympathy and understanding that

made splendid the life of Bishop Frank Weston in
East Africa, many generations later.

There is another fact of even greater significance with which I am more concerned here. It
will hardly be suggested that the England of
Elizabeth was distinguished for its piety. Sixteenth-century English Protestantism was, indeed,
far more national than religious. It inspired a
fervent hatred of Spain. It did not inspire any
obvious love of God. If it is to be assumed that
the spiritual character of the era is to be discovered
in the writings of its poets, then Elizabethan England was as pagan as the Florence of the Medicis
and the Rome of the Borgias. Puritanism was
something more than a revolt against ecclesias-
ticism and tradition. It was the revolt against
Erastianism, a protest against the doctrine, held
by Elizabeth, that it was the business of the Church
to bolster up the authority of the Crown, that the
Church was merely a highly important branch of
the Civil Service. I have no sort of sympathy with
the spirit of seventeenth-century Puritanism. But
its inspiration was, without question, the yearning
of the individual soul for direct and intimate association with the divine. As I understand it, the
Church was instituted primarily to make such
an association possible, to encourage spiritual

aspiration, to direct the pilgrim towards the Delectable Mountains, and to guide his steps so that he does not stumble on the way. The spread of Puritanism is the proof that the Church in England had lost any active realisation of the purpose for which it had been brought into being. One of the tragedies of history is that, owing to the break with Rome, England was entirely unaffected by the Counter-Reformation, by the enthusiasm of St. Vincent de Paul, by the preaching of St. Francis de Sales, by the mysticism of St. Teresa.

Spain was in every respect in striking contrast to England. From the beginning, the new learning was warmly welcomed to England by sovereigns and by prelates, and the Reformation was woven into a policy of national expansion. In the fourteenth century Spain was the home of learning, but its scholars were alien, its learning was exotic. With the expulsion and persecution of the Jews and the Moors, the glory of the Spanish universities departed. Cordova ceased to count in the intellectual life of Europe. Spain knew as little of the Renaissance as she knew of the Reformation. I do not minimise the loss. But Spain, behind its rampart of orthodoxy, was neither dying nor dead, intellectually or spiritually. The foundation of the Society of Jesus by the Spaniard St. Ignatius Loyola in 1540 was an event of immense significance in the history of Christendom. The writing of St. Teresa in *The Way of Perfection* was an event of no less importance. Here in obscurantist Spain, home of the Inquisition, the kingdom of the dull bigot, a woman of genius rediscovered how this corruptible can put on incorruption and this mortal can put on immortality. Personal religion was alive in Spain wherever else it may have appeared dead.

Teresa Cepeda y Ahumada was the daughter of a Castilian noble. She was born in the dour castle of Avila, which had been delicately ornamented by Moorish craftsmen and which had become the austere home of a rigid Christian family. There were books in plenty in the castle of Avila, religious books and tales of knight-errantry, and Teresa, the eldest of nine children, read them all, dreaming of adventure, thinking of herself, almost from her babyhood, as the servant of God. Her mother died while she was quite young, and she became the constant companion of her gloomy father, whom, in her invaluable popular study of the saint, Mrs. Cecil Chesterton has wittily described as " the forerunner of Sir Austen Feverel." Teresa was a beautiful, eager child, with dainty little hands and a strong, humorous mouth, not without her share of feminine vanity. She wrote in her *Life*:

" I began to make much of dress, to wish to please others by my appearance. I took pains with my hands and my hair, used perfumes and all vanities within my reach—and they were many, for I was very much given to them. I had no evil intention because I never wished anyone to offend God for me. This fastidiousness of excessive neatness lasted some years, and so also did other practices, which I thought then were not at all sinful. Now I see how wrong all this must have been."

As her brothers grew up, there was an abundance of young society at Avila and the suggestion of a love affair for the elder daughter of the house. But the experience brought fear and nothing more, and after her sister's marriage, Teresa was glad enough to leave home for the finishing of her education in an Augustinian convent. She wrote:

" I was already weary of myself and, though I offended God, I never ceased to have a great fear of Him, and contrived to go to confession as often as I could. I was very uncomfortable; but within eight days, I think sooner, I was much more contented than I had been in my father's house.

All the nuns were pleased with me; for the Lord
had given me the grace to please everyone wherever
I might be."

At the beginning, Teresa did not feel the slightest
inclination to take the veil. She was always extremely critical. She was always a realist, determined to recognise facts. The devotional practice
of the Augustinians seemed to her to be " over-
strained." The discipline was unintelligently
rigorous.

After eighteen months of the convent, Teresa
had a severe illness which left her an ailing woman
until the end of her long life, and it was during this
illness and after protracted mental and spiritual
contest that she determined to become a religious.
Her sister was amazed. Her father was indignant.
But Teresa was not to be turned from her purpose.
" Perhaps," says Mrs. Cecil Chesterton, " she perceived the doctrine, centuries later to be promul-
gated—the right of man and woman to life, liberty,
and the pursuit of happiness in the teeth of parental
opposition."

Teresa became a novice at the Carmelite Convent
of the Incarnation. The convent was poor. The
house was half in ruin. But the discipline was of
the lightest. After a year, Teresa was again very
ill and suffered horribly from the medical " science "

of the time.   In this second period of physical pain
she had her first experience of spiritual ecstasy.
She has herself described it:

" It is beyond the power of words to express or
describe the manner in which God draws close to
the soul, and the exceeding pain of it which deprives
her of consciousness; yet so sweet is this pain that
no delight of life can give more content.   The soul
would willingly be dying for ever of such a
hurt.   So dazed was I with this pain and glory
together, that I could not understand how it
could be."

Teresa was ill for three years.   During this time
she conceived her particular veneration for St.
Joseph, to whom she attributed her recovery and
whom she constantly invoked:

" I know not how any man can think of the
Queen of the Angels, during the time that she
suffered so much with the Infant Jesus, without
giving thanks to St. Joseph for the services he
rendered them then.   He who cannot find anyone
to teach him how to pray, let him take this glorious
saint for his master, and he will not wander out
of the way."

Teresa was now twenty-two, wan and thin, with
her eyes startlingly bright, and her tongue mor-
dantly witty.   The Carmelites of the Incarnation

were not enclosed. Their parlour was a popular
meeting place, and Teresa's clever talk was its chief
attraction. Her behaviour was above reproach,
but she began to feel that this life, half in the
world and half out of it, was utterly unsatisfactory.
Her father died. Four of her brothers were in
America. Another was a monk. She was alone
in the world, fated to fight a tremendous battle
without any family aid. Her confessors were
generally a hindrance rather than a help to her.
They were intellectually infinitely her inferiors.
They could never understand. Her increasing
resentment of the freedom of the parlour antago-
nised the nuns. She was accused of spiritual
pride. For eighteen years she lived obscurely,
unhappy, always bewildered, struggling towards
the light.

The reading of the *Confessions* of St. Augustine
was a landmark in her life. She identified herself
with the saint of Hippo. She began, herself, to
hear " the voice in the garden." Then, by good
fortune, she got into touch with one of the fathers
of the newly created Society of Jesus, who, with the
typical understanding of his Order, realised something of the greatness of the woman with whom
he had to deal and urged her to the violent and
complete subjugation of the body. Bodily morti-

fication brought with it, not unnaturally, the
"seeing of visions" and many moments of deep
despondency.

But her visions and her austerities excited suspicion and hostility. Individualism in religion
was not unreasonably feared. There was the
danger that she might be called before the Inquisition. But Teresa had grown sure of herself.
There is the spirit of St. Joan of Arc in her exclama-
tion: " Let all learned men rise up against me—let
the whole world persecute me—the evil spirits
torment me, but Thou, O Lord, fail me not. I
know the blessed rest of Thy deliverance for them
who trust only in Thee."

The yearning of the mystic was now fulfilled.
She had come constantly to hear the voice of God.
I write of the experiences of the mystic with the
proper hesitation of the normal man for whom such
ecstasy is an unknown territory of experience.
But no one but a professional sceptic can doubt its
reality. With her contemporary St. John of the
Cross, with whom she was later in her life to be in
close association, St. Teresa had linked herself with
the Eternal.

Teresa was not only a woman of prayer and contemplation. She was a woman of action. She was
a mystic, and she was an active and daring reformer.

Mr. A. C. Benson might have been thinking of the life of St. Teresa when he wrote in *The Thread of Gold* : " Neither of these great qualities, ardour and tranquillity, can stand alone; if we aim merely at enthusiasm, the fire grows cold, the world grows dreary, and we lapse into a cynical mood of bitterness and the vital flame burns low. Nor must we aim at mere tranquillity; for so we may fall into a mere placid acquiescence, a selfish inaction; our peace must be heartened by eagerness, our zeal calmed by serenity. If we follow the fire alone, we become restless and dissatisfied; if we seek only for peace, we become like the patient beasts of the field."

For years Teresa had endured the lazy, aimless, easy life of the Convent of the Incarnation. Now she could endure it no longer. Like St. Francis, she fell in love with Our Lady of Poverty. She determined to found a community, the first and most essential quality of which should be its poverty:

" Poverty is a strong wall. It is a wealth which includes all the wealth of the world; it is complete possession and dominion. What are Kings and Lords to me if I do not envy them their riches, nor seek to please them, if by so doing I should in the very least displease God ? What care I for honours,

7

if I know that the honour of a poor man dies in being poor?"

So, unarmed and unafraid, she started out on the last great crusade for a reformed and ennobled monasticism. She was growing old. She was feeble in health. But a big job had to be done, in face of opposition which she was far too intelligent to underestimate, and she set herself to it with a will. With infinite patience and address, she began to attract sympathy in high and influential places and to placate enmity. It must be remembered that the Council of Trent had urged monastic reform. It was the decadence of the religious life that had made the Reformation possible. It had excited the scorn of Rabelais and Erasmus. It had been the constant text of the preachers. Grossly exaggerated, it had been used as an excuse for the greed of Henry VIII. It is notable, too, that the Orders were the last possessions of the Church to be affected by the enthusiasm of the Counter-Reformation.

The opposition to Teresa was local, both lay and religious. From the first she was supported by the Jesuits and by certain earnest Dominicans, and finally she appealed to Rome. She stated her case clearly and unequivocally:

" A monastery of women unenclosed is, I believe,

the very greatest danger. Yea more, for those who will be wicked it is, I think, a road to hell, rather than a help to their weakness. . . . And all the while the poor things are not in fault; for they walk in the way that is shown them. Many of them are to be pitied; for they wished to withdraw from the world, and, thinking to escape from the dangers of it, and that they were going to serve our Lord, have found themselves in ten worlds at once, without knowing what to do, or how to help themselves."

Nuns must be poor, and they must be completely separate from the world. The rule of life must be severe, and it must be regularly followed. " Poverty, chastity and obedience " must be something more than a phrase.

Rome was sympathetic. The Baron Von Hügel has defended the Church's disinclination to approve novelty and its tendency to put the brake on reform. The character of the Church makes it vital that it shall move slowly. But Rome has often had its moments of courage and vision. One such moment was when the Pope instantly recognised the genius of St. Francis of Assisi. Another was the ready approval of the plans of St. Teresa. And very astute plans they were. Her Order was to follow the Carmelite rule, but the sisters were to be the " shoeless " Carmelites, the sisters of poverty, and it was essential that this new Convent of St. Joseph should be independent of the Carmelite Provincial. So Teresa planned to put it under the control of the Bishop of Avila, thus gaining the support of the secular clergy. Many difficulties had to be overcome, for Teresa herself was still subject to the jealous rule of the old foundation. But at last the convent was consecrated and housed, the first of St. Teresa's daughters wearing rough linen habits, with no shoes on their feet. It was a tiny community of thirteen women, but Teresa wrote: " I felt as if I were in bliss."

This was the beginning, but troubles were by no means over. Teresa was not herself a shoeless Carmelite. Her home was still in the Convent of the Incarnation, where the Prioress stormed and troubled and the sisters sniffed their disapproval. But public opinion was veering towards Teresa. New champions came, unsought, to her side, and at last, in 1563, Teresa was permitted to move to the home that she had founded. There she reinstated the rule decided in the thirteenth century: " Though the rule be somewhat severe—for we never eat meat except in cases of necessity, fast eight months in the year, and practise some other austerities besides, according to the primitive rule

—yet the sisters think it light on many points, and so they have other observances, which we have thought necessary for the more perfect keeping of it."

In her new home, Teresa de Jesus, as she was now called, demonstrated her intense practicality. She showed herself a first-rate cook. She insisted that the sisters should always be busy. When they were not praying, they must be spinning. Gushing personal friendships were forbidden, but sympathy was encouraged. She insisted on the duty of cleanliness. Discipline was insisted upon. St. Ignatius Loyola founded an Order of spiritual soldiers. Teresa had the same military ideal. Her sisters were soldiers, who " must always be on the alert to fulfil their Captain's orders, since it is He who pays them well for it."

In the years that followed the institution of St. Joseph's, Teresa wrote her *Life* and the *Way of Perfection*, in which she appeared as a great literary artist. There is humour in her writing, and a striking knowledge of human nature and particularly of women. She insists on the value of learning. Her soldiers must be instructed, they must know their jobs. What was their job? What was the object of the life, secluded behind a convent wall, shut away from the cares of this

world and the deceitfulness of riches? To attain
individual salvation? That, but only secondarily
and as a means to an end. Primarily it was, by
contemplation and austerity of life, to become
experts in prayer and then to offer instructed
prayer incessantly for the salvation of the world.
Whether or not it is worth while to spend a lifetime thus set apart and single minded, entirely
depends on the estimate of the value to the community of the prayers of the righteous.

Teresa lived quietly, writing, reading, praying
and ruling for five years. Then she again became
fervently busy. One small reformed establishment was not enough, and during the remaining
years of her life, despite ceaseless persecution and
opposition, and despite ever increasing physical
feebleness, she founded in all eleven reformed
Carmelite houses, six for women and five for
men.

That was her supreme achievement. A woman
in a country and an age of accepted masculine
superiority compelled men, by the sheer force of
inspired genius, to follow the example that she
had set. In her old age her monks were her
constant and loyal friends. They never failed her.
But her daughters, when the battles had been won,
became querulous and sometimes rebellious and

sorely wounded her great heart. But she never
for a moment lost her serenity.

The triumph of her life came in 1581, when,
by order of the Pope, the Carmelites who wore
shoes were permanently separated from those
who wore none. It was Rome that crowned her
life.

In 1582, Teresa started out on her last journey.
Archbishops were still sometimes tiresome. Prior-
esses were sometimes self-willed. But she had
won the hearts of the people. They crowded round
her, kissing her garments, and asking for her
blessing, as they had crowded round St. Thomas of
Canterbury as he landed on the Kentish coast on
his way to martyrdom, and as they were to crowd
round Laud on his way from Lambeth to the block.
But during her last journey the weather was dreadful. The roads were flooded. The cart in which
Teresa travelled was upset, and she was a dying
woman when she arrived at Alba. Here for days
she attended to the duties of her office and then,
still indomitable, she lay down quietly to die.
" The long road," says Mrs. Cecil Chesterton, " was
winding to its close; life's glorious adventure would
soon give place to death's discoveries."

She died on the morning of October 3rd, 1582, in
her sixty-seventh year. Her last admonition to

her followers was: "Pray for great desires, for out of them great benefits may come." Her last words on the earth were: "O my Lord, the longed-for hour has come at last; now we shall see one another."

St. Teresa was one of the greatest women of history, a great mystic, a great writer, a great reformer, a great administrator, a great cook—I find nothing of bathos in this description—gifted with humour, practical commonsense, unqualified patience and persistence, immense tact, fervent in business, serving the Lord.

Sixteenth-century Spain was the Spain of the Inquisition and the Armada, of Alva and Philip II. It was also the Spain of Don John of Austria, Cervantes and St. Teresa.

In 1614, St. Ignatius Loyola, St. Francis Xavier, the Jesuit Apostle of India, and St. Teresa were canonised together in St. Peter's in Rome.

In 1674, a lady, young, beautiful and broken-hearted, found refuge from the world with St. Teresa's daughters in their house in Paris. In the thirty years she lived there, at peace in her cold cell, Louise de la Vallière perhaps remembered the saint's words:

"Rank is of little worth, and the higher it is the greater the anxiety and trouble it brings," and,

" If a man be careful to please God continually,
and to hate the world, as he ought to do, I do not
see how he can be equally careful to please those
who live in the world."

QUEEN ELIZABETH

I HAVE already written a study of Queen Elizabeth, which with its companion volume, the *Story of the Renaissance*, was intended to be a brief popular retelling of the history of the sixteenth century, certainly the most interesting and important of all the centuries. There is little more that I can say than I have already said, and as I have written in my introduction, there is certainly nothing that anyone can add to Mr. Lytton Strachey's brilliant study of Elizabeth in the last years of her reign, when she had become " an old creature fantastically dressed, still tall, though bent, with hair dyed red above her pale visage, long blackening teeth, a high domineering nose, and eyes that were at once deep-set and starting forward—fierce, terrifying eyes, in whose dark blue depths something frantic lurked—something almost maniacal." This was Elizabeth when she was fifty-three !

Elizabeth was a Tudor, by far the most gifted of a remarkable family, but, in everything essential, the daughter of her father. She was vigorous of mind, and, despite hereditary disease, vigorous of body. She inherited " Bluff King Hal's " coarse mind and coarse tongue. She was immensely clever, with all her father's love of learning. She was the subtlest statesman of a subtle age. She used men and broke them as suited her purpose, and that purpose was to establish England as a great, if not the dominant, European power. She hated war. She believed that peace had greater victories than war. Yet her reign saw some of the greatest fights in English history. She lied, she intrigued, she plotted, always with one persistent end. And to that end she exploited her own personality. She was, above all other things, a political flirt.

Perhaps the only thing that is certain about her is that she knew quite well that, whether she married or not, she could never bear a child and that, therefore, the succession to the English throne could not remain with the Tudor family. She knew that she was the last of her family. Elizabeth never intended to marry, but, during more than half her long reign, she was persistently engaged in marriage negotiations, terrifying Spain by the suggestion that she should marry first Catherine de Medici's third son and then his younger

brother, with both of whom she carried on the most
outrageous flirtation, and ever and again letting it
be thought that she meant to marry Robert Dudley.

She and the Cecils invented the political doctrine
of the balance of power. Spain and France were
in constant contest for the domination of Europe.
It was Elizabeth's policy to prevent either of them
growing too strong. Her ambassadors were constantly whispering in Paris and in Madrid that
her support could be bought. Negotiations were
carried on, always with masterly delay, and at the
end they generally came to nothing.

The political situation had been immensely com-
plicated by the Reformation. When Elizabeth
succeeded her sister Mary, a large part of Germany,
the Low Countries, Switzerland and a considerable
part of France were Protestant. Philip of Spain
was the consistent soldier of the Church. His one
single-minded purpose was the extermination of
heresy and the recovery of the spiritual unity of
Europe. He has been described as " a merciless
bigot." But, alone among his contemporaries,
he was inspired by something more than personal
or national ambition.

During the reigns of the sons of Catherine de
Medici, France was torn by the wars of religion,
carried on by most irreligious persons on both sides,

and for years Catherine hesitated between Catholics and Huguenots, fearfully wondering whether to look to Paris and the De Guises or to the Protestants of the south to save the crown for the House of Valois. Elizabeth was always as "central-minded" and detached as Catherine de Medici was for a time. Such as it was, her personal religion was exactly her father's. She was a Catholic in belief. It would perhaps be truer to say that she was neither a Lutheran nor a Calvinist. She would never have even formally admitted direct Papal authority in her realm. But she hated the zeal of the Reformers, and she would, if she could, have kept the peace with Rome. It should always be remembered that it was not until 1570 that she was excommunicated, and that Rome began to encourage and approve the plots against her life and her throne. And one of the achievements of her reign for which she was personally responsible was saving the Church of England from both Rome and Geneva. It is historically untrue to say that the Church of England was the creation of the Elizabethan Settlement. That settlement preserved the Church from decadence into one of the countless Protestant sects. It preserved historical continuity. The revolt of the Puritans is sufficient proof of the accuracy of this assertion.

But though Elizabeth disliked Protestantism, she could not ignore the Protestant princes, nor could she altogether disregard that Protestant enthusiasm of a considerable proportion of her subjects which had first been excited by the Marian persecutions. She had constantly to resist the demand that England should put herself at the head of a Protestant confederation, the first purpose of which would be to drive the Spaniards from the Netherlands. Elizabeth feared that such a Protestant confederation would ensure the alliance of Spain and France, and for ten years she prevented any sort of official intervention. Then in 1585 came Leicester's expedition to Holland, with the death of Philip Sidney as its one dramatic incident and its inglorious end with quarrels between the English and the Dutch. During her reign there was constant fighting between the Spanish and the English. But the Elizabethan heroes who founded the British Empire were technically pirates. They sailed from Plymouth and from Bideford, equipped by private enterprise, almost always without the Queen's expressed approval. If they succeeded, she was always ready to take a full share of the plunder. But she was equally ready to disown and even to punish. It was the sailing of the Armada that brought Spain and England into acknowledged war.

Elizabeth was a princess of the Renaissance, not a princess of the Reformation. She loved learning and pageantry and magnificence. She was a man, and a very clever man, in her ambitions, and a woman, and a very silly woman, in her love of fulsome adulation. Always there must be a handsome flamboyant favourite on the steps of the throne. And she was viciously jealous. No other woman should give her favourites what she could not give. The story of Leicester's marriage is familiar, and Raleigh lost favour and place when he took a wife. To such a woman, the philanderings with a political purpose were an intense pleasure. The French princes, sent to England by their mother to woo the Virgin Queen, were sufficiently unattractive. The Duc d'Anjou, afterwards Henry III of France, was a particularly unpleasant fellow. The Venetian Envoy in Paris said of him:

" He is completely dominated by voluptuousness; covered with perfume and essences. He wears a double row of rings and pendants at his ears and spends vast sums on shirts and clothes. He charms and beguiles women by lavishing upon them the most costly jewels and toys."

But Elizabeth liked men who were fops, when they were not worse, and, in one of her letters, she declared that the over-scented and over-jewelled

Anjou was "worthy of the highest destiny the world could bestow."

In 1572, Elizabeth began her political flirtation with d'Alençon, d'Anjou's younger brother, and it continued until 1585. He was not at all prepossessing. "His pock-holes," wrote the British Ambassador in Paris, " are thick, but not great as are seen in some men whose faces are little disfigured with them if the visage and colour are otherwise liked. He was bashful and blushing at parting. His speech is not so fast as his brother's and he seems more advised. He is of 'stature mediocre.' "

In 1579, d'Alençon came to London. Elizabeth kissed him and petted him in public as was her wont, and christened him " her little frog." But there she stopped. There was a formal demand for her hand two years later, but she was ready with excuses and demands for delay, and, with great relief, the Spanish Ambassador reported: " The Queen is simply procrastinating to draw the French into a defensive alliance without burdening herself with a husband," and wise old Catherine de Medici said to the Venetian Envoy in Paris: " Queen Elizabeth is very artful, and my son is very young." The English people detested the idea of a French marriage, and Elizabeth was always affected by

8

public opinion. The "little frog" was sent home, and the Queen dropped into poetry:

> I grieve, yet dare not show my discontent;
> I love, and yet am forced to seem to hate;
> I dote, but dare not what I ever meant;
> I seem stark mute, yet inwardly do prate;
> I am, and am not—freeze, and yet I burn;
> Since from myself my other self I turn.

D'Anjou and d'Alençon were more than a little terrified by the tempestuous red-headed woman to whom their mother insisted that they should pay court, and mightily relieved when the marriage negotiations came to nothing. But there is no question of the genuine adoration felt for Elizabeth, in her old age, by her own countrymen. No sovereign has ever dazzled her subjects as Elizabeth dazzled sixteenth-century England. No woman has ever excited such exaggerated romantic admiration. This has been expressed, with no great exaggeration, by Charles Kingsley in the fantastic hyperbole that he puts in the mouth of Frank Leigh in *Westward Ho!*

In February, 1587, Mary Stuart was beheaded in Fotheringhay Castle. For nearly nineteen years the most unfortunate of all royal ladies had been a prisoner in England. She had crossed the Solway Firth, hoping for her cousin's protection against her rebellious subjects. She became, to an extent against her own shrewd judgment, the hope of the English Roman Catholic party. Elizabeth was to be removed, and Mary, her legal heiress, was to reign in her place. It is probable that Elizabeth, herself, never took the plots very seriously. She was no coward, and most of the plots were banal when they were not obviously inspired by an *agent provocateur*. But Protestant fervour increased as Elizabeth's reign went on, and in the Protestant popular mind Mary was the agent of the King of Spain and the Pope of Rome, the enemy of England and England's Queen. There was a growing clamour for her death, and very reluctantly Elizabeth agreed. Certainly she had no love for Mary. Ugly women rarely admire beautiful women. But there was the tie of blood between them, and moreover Elizabeth was a good trade unionist. Queens should stand by queens in a changing world. But circumstances were too much for her. On the face of it the execution was a political blunder. If Mary had not been beheaded in 1587 it is unlikely that the Spanish Armada would have sailed in 1588. But if the Armada had not sailed, to be destroyed veritably by the grace of God, Elizabeth's reign would have lost its chief glory.

A few months after Mary's death, Robert

Devereux, Earl of Essex, came to court. He was a young man of twenty-one, handsome, rich and well-born. Robert Devereux came of a family bound by blood ties to the Queen, and his stepfather was Robert Dudley, Earl of Leicester, himself for years the royal favourite, who has been described as "that luxuriant, creeping, flaunting, all-pervading existence which struck its fibres into the mould and coiled itself through the whole fabric of Elizabeth's life and reign." Essex was a typical aristocrat of the late Renaissance. He could write grammatical Latin. He could compose tolerable English verse. He excelled in manly sports. He had seen military service with his stepfather in the Netherlands. He was high-spirited, romantic, and, with his fair hair and tall thin figure, admirably good-looking.

Essex had been deliberately brought to Court by the Leicester party to supplant Walter Raleigh, who had supplanted Leicester. Raleigh had every advantage over Essex except youth. He was six feet in height, with a dark curling moustache and beard. He had wit, a plausible tongue, personal fascination, and a great reputation as an adventurer. Major Hume has described him as " a great genius, whose knowledge was encyclopædic, and whose busy brain was teeming with far-reaching plans for giving England a noble share in the new-found lands beyond the sea." In 1587, he was Her Majesty's Captain of the Guard. Elizabeth had made him rich. He owned great estates and many monopolies. He was at the very zenith of his influence. But he was ten years older than Essex, and, before midsummer, it was reported of the Queen, "when she is abroad nobody is near her but my Lord of Essex; and at night my Lord is at cards or one game or another with her till the birds sing in the morning."

The Queen was fascinated by her new playfellow, and the boy behaved to her with an excess of inso-lence which the Queen had never tolerated before. While he was in attendance on her during one of her progresses in Hertfordshire, he wrote to a friend of the Queen's continued affection for Raleigh:

" I spake, what of grief and choler, as much against him as I could: and I think that he, standing at the door (as Captain of the Guard), might very well hear the worst that I spoke of himself. In the end I saw she was resolved to defend him and cross me. . . . For myself, I told her, I had no joy to be in any place, but was loth to be near about her when I knew my affection so much thrown down, and such a wretch as Ralegh highly esteemed of her. . . . This strange alteration is by Ralegh's means, and the Queen, who hath tried all other ways, now will whether she can by these hard courses drive me to be friends with Ralegh, which shall rather drive me to many other extremities."

It is clear that the young ambitious courtier was, from the beginning, bored to death by the constant running after a woman whom, wonderful though she may have been, he had never seen " until her neck had grown scraggy, her bosom withered, her cheeks wrinkled, and her coiffure a red wig." He was giving her the joy of his youth and good looks, which he certainly did not underestimate, and he was bold enough to believe that he knew how to manage a woman whom no man had ever managed. " My Lord Essex had a sort of set opinion that the Queen should be brought to nothing but by a kind of necessity or authority." The whole story of this last love affair of Elizabeth is pitiful in its unpleasant stupidity. The Queen had always bullied her lovers and they had trembled. Essex defied her. When she sent him away, he was only too glad to go, and it was with the greatest difficulty that he was persuaded to return.

The Armada sailed and was destroyed. Essex had none of the glory of the great fight. But he insisted on accompanying the expedition that delivered the counter-attack on the coast of Spain, and he sailed without Elizabeth's knowledge. She was furious. She wanted her lap dog at home. But the expedition was of little consequence, the absence of Essex was short, and he was soon restored to his old favour. The Queen paid his debts. She gave him the right to farm the custom duties on sweet wines imported into the country. She was complacent enough to allow him to marry. She was growing too old to care.

In 1591, Essex was permitted to command an expeditionary force sent to France to fight with the Huguenots against the Catholic Leaguers. He never showed the smallest capacity as a general, but he never failed in romantic gestures.

Leicester was now dead. William Cecil was very old, and in the last years of Elizabeth the English figure of greatest interest and by far the greatest accomplishment was Francis Bacon, that man of many gifts, of great learning, and of no scruples. Raleigh was disgraced and in prison, and allying himself with Bacon, Essex was called to the Council and began to play at statesmanship, as he had already played at soldiering, and not without a certain astuteness.

Essex was a loyal friend, and it was care for the interests of his friend that was the beginning of his troubles with his mistress. He urged that Bacon

should be appointed to the vacant position of
Attorney-General. Bacon was up to his eyes in
debt, and the office was an extremely lucrative one.
Essex had grown very sure of himself. He believed
that the old Queen was his puppet. He had persuaded himself that he had only to ask to receive.
But Elizabeth was still Elizabeth, the woman who
delighted in promising and not fulfilling. More
than once Essex left the Court in sulky rage at not
having his own way, promptly tearfully to be called
back and then to be roundly abused. Pettings
followed abuse, and Essex was again confident of
success. But in the end he lost, and Edward Coke
was made Attorney-General. This was a great
victory for the Cecils, who had backed his candida-
ture, and a sore humiliation for the favourite. As
it happened, the Solicitor-Generalship was also
vacant, and Essex determined that if not one, then
the other should be Bacon's. But two and a haJ
years passed, and again Essex failed. The Queen
would play the fool, but never with affairs of State.

Failing in the Council, Essex once more turned
his mind to the field. He persuaded the Queen to
put him in command of a second expedition, which
sailed from Plymouth to attack the coast of Spain.
The expedition had little practical result, and
while Essex was away from England, his enemy,

the humpbacked Robert Cecil, was installed by the Queen as her Secretary of State. When he returned, Essex had a chilly reception. The Queen was annoyed that her money had been wasted, and she was extremely jealous of the popular acclaim given to Essex for his victory at Cadiz. Gloriana brooked no rival. Her years of sovereignty were drawing to an end. She knew that. The Tudor era was closing in. But while she lived, all the prerogatives and all the glory of the Crown should be hers alone. At the first council meeting that he attended the Queen was sarcastic, and Cecil asked unpleasant questions. But good looks triumphed once more. The old amorist supplanted the angry sovereign and the royal favour was restored. But the silent Robert Cecil watched and waited in patience.

Bacon, who realised that his own fortunes were bound up with those of his patron, saw the danger of the situation. He understood the Queen far better than Essex. He knew that pacifism was the key of her statesmanship. He knew that vanity was her dominating personal quality. So he advised Essex to walk warily, to be submissive to the royal lady's whims, to take particular care always to be dandified in his appearance when in the royal presence, to keep himself well in hand.

But Essex had no self-control. He was something of an artist in his impetuosity, and he was always impatient of convention. Day after day attendance at Court became infinitely tiresome. He yearned for change and freedom.

Early in 1597, another naval attack on Spain was planned, and Essex, who had recently been made Master of the Ordnance, was again put in command, having the additional satisfaction of having Raleigh under his orders. The result was worse disaster. The fleet sailed from Plymouth almost to be destroyed by a tremendous south-westerly gale. Essex and Raleigh quarrelled, and Essex returned to England with a few small Spanish cargo ships as the only return for the expenditure of money which Elizabeth always grudged. She thoroughly disliked these semi-piratical expeditions against the Spaniards. They could only be excused when they paid.

This time she was the more annoyed because Essex's popularity was unabated. She knew quite well that he was neither general nor admiral, and her sense of justice was outraged when she found that this new failure was attributed by the people to the weather and to Walter Raleigh. Flattering letters did something to appease her, but having written them, Essex badly blundered. He resented the promotion that had been given to his rivals during his absence, and instead of hurrying to the Court, he sulked at his country house. The sulking appeared to pay, for when at last he returned, he received the signal honour of being made Earl Marshal of England.

In the winter of 1598, Essex remained at Court consoling himself, in the intervals of attendance on Gloriana, with flirtations with her ladies which, of course, the astute eyes of Elizabeth did not fail to notice; but by now she seems to have grudgingly admitted to herself that youth must be served. He made things worse by opposing the Cecils, with whom the Queen always agreed, urging that England should make the alliance with Holland and Protestant Germany against France and Spain which Elizabeth had fought against for years. On one occasion he lost his temper in the Council Chamber and was actually insulting to the Queen. She said nothing. He wrote her a letter couched in curiously offensive terms. There was no answer. He hurried to Whitehall and was not admitted. His friends urged him to apologise and ask for pardon, and Bacon, now convinced that Essex was riding for a fall, brought their intimacy to an end.

But Essex still had friends, and very dangerous

ones. He was popular in the City of London,
which regarded him as the champion of Protestantism. He was elected Chancellor of the University of Cambridge. He believed, and not unreasonably, that if he stayed away long enough,
Gloriana would repent and that he would recover
favour without humiliation.

There was trouble in Ireland, serious trouble, and
Essex, who still attended the royal Council, vehe-
mently insisted that he was the one man who could
pacify the country, and demanded that he should
be appointed Lord Deputy. And the Queen consented. London again acclaimed him as he passed
through the City before embarking, and again the
Queen was not pleased. The job was too great for
the new Lord Deputy's abilities. He had many
small victories in Ireland and many picturesque
progresses, but three months passed, his army was
deplorably weakened, and the rebellion was not
even scotched. Essex grew ill and frightened. He
wrote to the Queen, complaining that he had not
sufficient support and blaming others for his
failure. Elizabeth sent reinforcements with a curt
letter. At home Francis Bacon was whispering in
the royal ear that, charming and ornamental as
Essex was as a courtier, he was hopeless as a
general. And in Dublin Essex knew that if he

obeyed the royal orders and marched into Ulster complete defeat would be the inevitable consequence. This time he thoroughly lost his head. He would take his army back to England, stir up the extreme Protestantism of London, drive the Cecils from power, and compel the Queen to act according to his advice. The lover was in revolt. He had dreams of the crown. The Queen must die soon. Would not England choose Robert Devereux before James Stuart?

But the hot mood did not continue for long. He was far from well. He recalled the Queen's moments of anger. He had his doubts about Cecil. He determined to obey the orders from London, at least in part. He interviewed the leader of the Irish rebels, patched up a peace which really meant a rebel triumph, and then hurried home and, fearful of what would happen, rushed into the royal presence, mud-bespattered and in his riding-boots, to find the Queen in her dressing-gown and without wig. And this mysterious woman was rather flattered, receiving him without protest and dismissing him with a smile.

When they met a few hours afterwards, she now berouged, and he brushed and properly clad, the Queen had become the hard-headed statesman. She had talked over the Irish situation with Cecil.

She had realised the blow to her prestige involved in the treaty that Essex had signed. She was cold and inquisitive. She was deadly critical, and the next day Essex was imprisoned at York House in the Strand.

Essex was very ill, but he was cited before the Star Chamber for disobeying royal orders in Ireland. Nothing happened for a year, and then Essex, who had recovered his health, began actually to plot against the Queen with the Irish and the Scotch. It was all exceedingly stupid, the plottings of a hare-brained, disappointed adventurer, all of course promptly reported to Cecil. Still Elizabeth hesitated. Her affection for her handsome favourite was by no means dead. In her own odd way, she loved him, and it was impossible for her to fear him. She wanted to punish him, to humiliate him, and that was all. Again he appeared before the Star Chamber, Bacon being one of his accusers. The Earl prayed for mercy and was ordered to return to his house and to stay there during the Queen's pleasure. Letter after letter was written begging for complete forgiveness. He was granted one interview which ended in a quarrel, and then his monopolies were taken away from him. " When horses become unmanageable, it is necessary to tame them by stinting them in the quantity

of their food!" she said. The loss of income in-
furiated Essex. "The Queen's conditions," he ex-
claimed, "are as crooked as her carcass," and the
remark was repeated. And the hunchback still
listened and waited.

There were whispers in the City that Cecil was
plotting with the Spaniards, that Raleigh was
planning the assassination of Essex. There was talk
of deposition, and at last there was a rising in
London which, as a matter of fact, was little more
than a quickly quelled riot. It resulted in the
arrest of Essex and his trial for treason, with
Bacon as Crown prosecutor. The trial was a farce.
Essex defended himself cleverly and with dignity,
but when he was condemned to death and sent to
the Tower, he lost his courage and grovelled. He
still hoped that the Queen would relent. But she
who revelled in hesitation and delighted in half-
measures, this time acted with relentless swiftness.
Essex was condemned on February 19th and exe-
cuted on the 25th. The story of the ring which,
sent to the Queen, might have saved his life, but
was intercepted by one of his enemies, is almost
certainly untrue. Essex was beheaded privately
early in the morning, and Walter Raleigh stood at
the foot of the scaffold.

Elizabeth's personal vanity was great. Her love

of dominance was greater. When that was threatened, she ceased to be the doting middle-aged woman. She had come to realise that her position as the sole master of England was being imperilled by the public flouting of her authority. While Essex was by her side, it was easy to forgive his boyish waywardness. When he was away from her, failing in his command and deliberately disobeying orders, until at last circumstances compelled him into actual rebellion, there was always Robert Cecil to suggest the consequences of weakness, with Francis Bacon, not far away, eager to secure royal favour by playing the traitor to his friend.

She consented to the execution with genuine sorrow and reluctance. " If I could have spared the life of this ungrateful and perfidious Essex and secured the continuance of my authority in the State, I would gladly have been lenient," she wrote, " but you yourself have seen that he was unworthy; and while he lived I could not live, and I was compelled to rid myself of this danger. But I confess that I have been partly to blame for this misfortune, as I had made too much of Essex, and had allowed him to become greater among the nobility and the common people than was desirable for a subject."

The death of Essex was a blow from which the Queen never recovered. She retained something of her energy and a good deal of her temper, but there was no more zest in living, and death, when it came two years later, came as a relief.

" The night before her death, Whitgift, the Archbishop of Canterbury, endeavoured to console her by recalling her great achievements, and the dying Queen said with admirable good sense and humour: ' My Lord, the Crown which I have borne so long has given enough of vanity in my time. I beseech you not to augment it in this hour when I am so near my death.'

" So died Elizabeth Tudor in the seventieth year of her life and the forty-fifth year of her reign."

ON a spring morning in the year 1674, Louise de la Vallière, mistress of Louis XIV of France and a duchess in her own right, quietly left the Palace of Versailles for the convent of Mount Carmel in the Faubourg Saint-Jacques under the shadow of the Cathedral of Notre Dame. Here she was to spend thirty years in penance and prayer. No woman in the long line of kings' mistresses was ever more single-minded or ever more in love with her lover. The gentle, diffident, pathetic Louise left Versailles, and the gorgeous Athenaïs, Marquise de Montespan, reigned in her stead. Indeed, the two women had reigned together for some years, sharing the King's favours with constant humiliation for the gentle Louise. Saint-Simon says that de Montespan was " as beautiful as the dawn." She was witty, audacious, seductive, a miracle of grace. She was a great seventeenth-century lady with no morals and with admirable taste.

In 1674, Louis was a man of thirty-six, and France, which had been under his personal rule for thirteen years, had become the dominant power in Europe. Louis XIV was a man of many admirable qualities. He was charming and dignified, kindly and even-tempered. He showed consistently good judgment in selecting his ministers and generals. He had learned caution from Cardinal Mazarin, and his famous " I will see " indicates his habit of careful consideration before arriving at every important decision. He was handsome, energetic, and though he had his full share of illness and disease, he was a man of iron constitution. Louis XIV was King of France. That does not mean that he regarded himself as the steward of his people or that he ever supposed that it was his business to safeguard their interests and to ensure their prosperity and content. France was his personal estate for which, in a vague way, he was responsible to God, but which was his to do what he would with. As has been said, the bishops were his chaplains, the Finance Minister his cashier, the generals his servants. France was the King and remained the King until his death.

This conception of his position, with the continuous success of his diplomacy and his armies, filled Louis with a fantastic vanity which was stimulated by the army of courtiers who surrounded him in the Palace of Versailles. He was their god.

His life was spent in what to most men would have been an intolerable atmosphere of etiquette and ceremony, duke intriguing against duke as to who should have the privilege of handing the King his shirt. Louis was not intelligent enough for any sort of self-criticism, but constant servility from eight o'clock in the morning till midnight sometimes bored even him, and the beautiful, witty, reckless de Montespan supplied a welcome relief. She was a gambler and a spendthrift. That the King did not mind. She was arrogant, and at times she even dared to bully her royal lover, and this must have been a pleasant and novel experience.

When he was twenty-one, the King married the Spanish princess Marie Thérèse, who was, says M. Jacques Boulenger, " a pattern all her life long of the most solid virtue and the greatest stupidity." When the young bride and bridegroom drove together through the streets of Paris, a certain Mme. Scarron was among the spectators, moved, as they all were, by the King's good looks and gallant bearing. " I do not believe anything so handsome can be seen anywhere," she wrote to one of her friends, " and the Queen must have gone to bed well pleased with her husband." Little, on that fine morning, did Mme. Scarron dream how large a part she was destined to play in the King's life.

Françoise d'Aubigné, Mme. Scarron in 1660, but who lives in history as Mme. de Maintenon, was born on November 28th, 1635. Her father was a Huguenot. Her mother, who was nearly thirty years his junior, was a pious Catholic, and their marriage took place in a prison in Bordeaux where d'Aubigné, a thoroughgoing swashbuckler, was incarcerated for a petty debt. Eight years afterwards Françoise was born in another prison, the Conciergerie at Niort near Tours, where her father was again in trouble. Françoise was born into perplexity and disgrace. Her father was merely a nominal Protestant, though her grandfather had been one of the great Huguenot leaders. D'Aubigné cared nothing about his daughter's religion and she was baptised a Catholic, but her father was constantly in trouble and her mother was harassed by poverty and debt, and the girl was brought up by a Protestant aunt, who soon wearied of her charge, and Françoise was sent to an Ursuline convent and was converted to the Church into which she had been baptised, though, young as she was, she made the condition that she should not be forced to believe that her aunt was in a state of damnation. From that time the Catholic religion was the dominating influence in her life. Her girlhood remained poor and shabby. She was snubbed

by her rich relations. She was one of the un-
wanted. And when she was sixteen, she married.
" I preferred marriage to going into a convent,"
she explained in after years. Her husband was
certainly undesirable. Mme. Saint-René Taillandier says:

" There dwelt in Paris, just at that time, a
poverty-stricken man of letters, of a droll wit, a
feeling heart, and an infirm body, who deadened
his misery by presiding over a coterie of wits and
makers of merry quips. He had that caustic form
of humour which has been denominated ' the
hunchback's wit.' Yet this man, this poet, this
Scarron, was no hunchback, nor even, as has been
so often said, a legless cripple. He was a poor
paralysed creature who spent his days in a jointed
armchair, shut in beneath hinged panels. Enclosed after this fashion, he was like some huge
beetle in its carapace. When night came, he was
taken out of his box and put to bed. Nobody had
ever seen more of him than his head that always
hung on one side, and his big prominent eyes that
looked different ways. He provided amusement
for his acquaintances, and subsisted on the scanty
sums his poems brought him in, and small gifts
bestowed by friendly hands. Much indulgence
was shown to the somewhat risky flights of his

poetic muse. Certain pious and extremely high-born ladies, grave dowagers whose virtue was not affrighted by the entertaining fancies of the witty, were assiduous in their attendance round his arm-chair. Now and then, in the midst of his peals of laughter, Scarron would cry out sharply from sheer pain, and the ladies about him were thus able, all at once, to enjoy the gay wit of the poet, and taste the pleasure of pitying, and even of loving a little, a poor wretch who was as unfortunate as he was entertaining."

Scarron had a pension and a more or less assured small income, and despite the fact that he was forty-two and diseased, the young girl of sixteen married him, quite content, for want of better occupation, "to help an invalid to live a decent life and die a worthy death."

The marriage took place in the year when the power of the French monarchy, or rather of Maz-arin, Minister of the Queen Regent, Anne of Austria, and probably her husband, was threatened by the rebellion of the Fronde, that amazing conspiracy which Dumas makes at least half intelligible. Hatred and jealousy of the Italian Mazarin was the motive of a revolt that lasted for four years, that enlisted "all petty and frustrated ambitions," and which was inspired by such futilities as to whether Mgr. de Retz was to have a Cardinal's hat and Mme. de Longueville was to sit by the Queen's side.

Scarron had been received by the Queen and was impressed, as everyone was, by her kindly graciousness. The Cardinal was ready to be his patron, but his pen was bought by the Queen's enemies. He delighted fashionable Paris with witty lampoons of the Cardinal, with the result that he lost a royal pension and for a while he and his young wife had a very lean time. But thanks to her charm and gravity—she was genuinely shocked by the coarse jokes of the poet and his friends—patrons were found again. Fat capons were left at Scarron's door, which he ate even on the Fridays of Lent while Madame sat at the end of the table " picking a herring." Gradually, too, Madame became the hostess of a salon, perhaps the most intellectual in Paris. Madame de Sévigné, the famous letter-writer, was her frequent visitor as was the even more famous Ninon de l'Enclos, the mistress of many lovers, already a woman of forty, who was to live to be ninety and to know Voltaire when he was a schoolboy. But even with capons in the larder, the Scarron purse was often empty, and the poet's wife's life was one long anxiety.

Scarron died in 1660, leaving his widow, when his

debts had all been punctiliously paid, with less
than five thousand francs. " I am not fated to be
happy," she wrote to her uncle, " but we devout
folk call such trials the visits of the Lord." Her
piety was genuine, but she was shrewd enough,
while maintaining patience and dignity, to cultivate
influential friends. She was well born and well
educated, and soon after her husband's death, and
thanks to the good offices of the Queen Mother, a
small pension was granted " the young, virtuous,
and very intelligent widow." She was a welcome
guest at fashionable parties, where her character
was admired and her wit appreciated. She made
herself useful in a thousand ways, now arranging
the details of a wedding, now running a country
house for a great lady. " Six o'clock in the morning never found me in bed," she wrote, " while my
friends never got up till noon."

After a time her religion became more austere
and her wit less entertaining. One sprightly Abbé
confessed that he found her a bore, and Paris society
began to wonder if the widow Scarron were not too
good to be true. Much scandal has been written of
her years between 1660 and 1670, but most of it
after Françoise had become the power behind the
throne and by the people who hated her. What
is almost certainly the truth was told by the aged

and wicked Ninon. " Madame Scarron was always correct in her conduct. She was not fitted for love. She was virtuous out of weak-mindedness. I tried to cure her, but she was too much afraid of God." But for all her troubles and for all her piety, Mme. Scarron at thirty-five was not without her attraction. " She did not set up to be a beauty," said Mme. Scudéry, " though she had a thousand obvious charms." She dressed simply but well. Her manners were perfect.

In 1670, Mme. Scarron was introduced to de Montespan. The favourite had just become the mother of a girl baby whose father was the King, and she decided that Mme. Scarron was the ideal person to become its guardian. Her discretion was notorious, her breeding was without question, and accordingly she was entrusted with the care of the little girl and of the boy who followed. She attended to their well-being with the most affectionate care and was repaid, particularly by the little Duc de Maine, the best loved of all the King's children, with almost idolatrous affection. Mme. Scarron felt that she had been chosen by divine providence for a great mission. It was for her to bring up the royal children as good Catholics. It was for her, sooner or later, to convert Mme. de Montespan. It might even be for her to persuade the King himself to better ways. Her position was certainly anomalous, for this austere Catholic was in effect the accomplice of an adulterous relation. But the end justified the means.

It was long before the King felt any sort of interest in the grave, sober, self-satisfied governess. But he was an affectionate father. The children were often taken to Saint-Germain—there became seven of them in all—and after the Parliament had agreed to their legitimisation, the governess and her charges went to live in the palace. Mme. Scarron's position was now still more delicate, but it was made more tolerable by the fact that the King promised her a present of 100,000 francs ! After worrying delay—Louis would never be hurried—the gift was forthcoming and doubled when the King learned of her solicitous care for the Duc de Maine, and with the money grant she received the title of Mme. de Maintenon.

It must not be supposed that the King's flagrant love-makings, with mistress after mistress installed in the royal palace, passed without protest. So long as his mother lived, indeed, for to her he never lacked in affection and respect, there was at least some discreet pretence. But after her death *le roi soleil* openly did what was pleasing to himself. The King could do no wrong.

He showed the smallest regard for the Queen. Her stupidity wearied him, and she was compelled to accept both Louise de la Vallière and de Montespan among her ladies-in-waiting. For the Church the King had more regard and not a little fear, and the Church did not lack courage in its denunciation of his infidelities.

The great preacher Bossuet, to whom Louise de la Vallière owed her conversion, made open and public appeals to Louis to reform his ways, and the priest chosen to preach to the Court on Easter Day, 1675, in the chapel of the palace of Saint-Germain, was even more outspoken. Mme. de Montespan was seated just behind the King, to whom the preacher said: " How many conversions, Sire, would be brought about by your example! What a charm might it not work on certain disheartened sinners who have fallen back in despair, if they could say to themselves, ' Behold this man whom we have seen in the same debauchery as our own, behold him now converted and submitting himself to God '! " The sermon was described by Mme. de Sévigné as " the great Pan's thunderclap." The King listened and made no comment. His mistress was frightened and furiously angry.

After Easter, the King joined his army in Flanders, and de Montespan was left at home to read parts of the Scriptures suggested to her by Bossuet and to pretend an imitation penitence. But by the summer Louis had forgotten the Easter sermon, and his mistress was restored to favour. But not for long. The King began to have new fancies. His mistress's sarcasms no longer amused him. He was growing weary of her extravagance.

In 1680, several of the courtiers at Versailles died of poisoning. A wretched woman called Voisin was arrested and, under torture, declared that de Montespan had not only bought love philtres from her by which she hoped to retain the King's favour, but that she had also bought poisoned gloves for the removal of her rivals. The King was disgusted. Long before, there had been rumours at Versailles that de Montespan had shared in the orgies of the Black Mass and that she had sold her soul to the devil. But these were just rumours, probably untrue. The woman Voisin had supplied more definite evidence against her. The King was only forty-two, but he was growing old, and with increasing years and sexual satiety his conscience began to prick him as in such circumstances conscience often does. De Montespan was dangerous. He was no longer indifferent to the admonitions of the Church, and, moreover, the quiet influence of the governess of the royal bastards had been steadily increasing. And de Montespan was dismissed, this time for ever.

Mme. de Maintenon had been at Court for ten years. De Montespan had bitterly resented the King's interest in her governess, and the two women had constantly bickered, de Montespan violently, de Maintenon with chilly dignity. The King's bounty had made her independent, and the squabbles always finished with de Maintenon expressing the intention at once to leave the Court. She was not allowed to go. In all probability she had no intention to go. She had become a power, the King had grown into the habit of consulting her, and honourable and sincere as she was, she enjoyed her power. The Church rejoiced at her ever increasing influence and looked to her to protect the King against himself. De Montespan's fascination had passed, but there were other women at Versailles, younger than she and as good-looking, who were more than ready to succeed her. De Maintenon was naturally unpopular with these Court beauties. To them she was " tiresome and insistent; she did not understand." But the Queen, the dull-witted, neglected Marie Thérèse, was her friend.

Long before 1684, the foreign Ambassadors had

realised that there was a new and unexpected development at the Court of the most Christian King and that " the good-looking lady in a black gown," always modestly in the background, was becoming a most potent influence affecting the life of the King and, indirectly, because she was never a politician, the policy of France. Her official position was now Lady of the Bedchamber to the wife of the Dauphin, a plain, well-intentioned Bavarian princess who loved books, music and a quiet life. And the Lady of the Bedchamber was a figure of so great importance that Pope Innocent XII sent her a brief written with his own hand. The governess of the royal bastards now governed the royal family.

As her position became more important, her popularity increased. She asked for nothing for herself. She asked nothing for her relations. She had no personal ambition. She was " honestly fond of quiet, embroidery, the education of young girls and meditation." The King's salvation was her one passion. She became embroiled in public affairs against her will, and, so far as the King was concerned, she was not fighting for herself as the other women of Versailles had fought, she was fighting for the Queen, and the Queen knew it.

Mme. de Maintenon regarded herself as the ser-

vant of the Church. As her biographer says, "she
belonged with all the strength of her being, and by
a secret vow, as it were, to a living and spiritual
organisation, the members of which were all
passionately intent on the realisation of one great
end, the establishment of moral order, labouring to
that end, working for it as it worked for them, and
doing all this openly, not secretly."

The conversion of Louis XIV has often been regarded, and not without justification, as merely
due to weariness, as the inevitable reaction against
excess. But it is interesting and important to
note that while the England of the Restoration and
the Church of the Restoration were little outraged
by the excesses of Charles II—I do not forget that
Ken refused to provide a lodging for Nell Gwynne—
the unreformed Church in France strove valiantly
and successfully to bring the immorality of Versailles to an end. It is true, of course, that the
more or less dignified intrigues of Louis XIV were
followed by the vulgar debaucheries of the Regency
and of the reign of Louis XV. But that does not
affect the religious fervour of the later seventeenth
century.

Among the Court ladies, only Madame the second
wife of the King's unpleasant brother—his first wife
was the delicious Henrietta of England, daughter

of Charles I—hated de Maintenon. To this typical German princess she was an " old slut," an " old witch." Years afterwards her libels were repeated by Saint-Simon in his Diary, but they are obviously nothing more than the vicious babblings of a jealous and ill-tempered woman.

On one occasion a letter from Madame to one of her German relatives was opened in the Post Office, as Saint-Simon says, "according to the usual custom."   In it she referred to Mme. de Maintenon as "this piece of filth," and Saint-Simon says:— " The officials who examined it found it so strong that they did not content themselves, as usual, with taking extracts, but sent the original to the King." Then there was trouble, and Madame was reduced to apologies and tears.   But her hatred continued. Indeed, her only place in French history is that she was the only active enemy that de Maintenon ever made.

The conversion of Louis was effected before the death of the Queen in 1683, but his religion was more formal than sincere.   De Maintenon herself admitted: " The King never misses a Station or a penance, but he cannot understand the necessity of humbling himself and acquiring the true spirit of repentance."   And M. Boulenger says that the King's religion was "inspired less by love than by the fear of hell and the hope of Paradise which he thought that Heaven would certainly grant him provided he attended Divine Service assiduously, observed Lent and, in short, gave God His due and paid respectful court to the Almighty."

But Louis wore his religion with an air, and the whole atmosphere of Versailles was changed. Intrigue came to an end. Love was taboo. The whole Court fasted throughout Lent. Theatrical entertainments practically came to an end. " The courtier of the past had flowing hair, was dressed in doublet and hose, wore wide boots, and was a libertine," says La Bruyère. " This is no longer the mode: he now wears a wig, a closely fitting coat, plain stockings, and is devout." Besides being devout, the courtier was exceedingly uncomfortable. As the King grew older, he grew economical and suspicious. Everyone's letters were opened and read. Fires were forbidden. The courtiers froze as they prayed.

The Queen died, and immediately the Church party determined that the King must marry again. He was much too susceptible to be allowed the freedom of a widower. His mistresses had been discarded. He had repented of his sins. But he might well sin again. But whom was he to marry ? The answer obviously was " the lady who lived the life of a hermit at Versailles," who was then forty-eight, three or four years the King's senior. She was his confidante. He trusted her intelligence. He had been influenced by her faith, and though the marriage was never made public, there is no question that it took place, Voltaire thinks in 1685, but probably even earlier than that.

Voltaire has called the marriage a marriage of conscience, and certainly de Maintenon had little to gain by it. She was passionless, middle-aged, and she knew the King through and through. " No woman," says Mme. Saint-René Taillandier, " falls in love with a man on whose actions she has been passing judgment for fifteen years." Her formal position hardly changed at all. The marriage was kept secret. She was never publicly recognised as the Queen Consort, and Voltaire says that the only mark of distinction that she accepted was that, at Mass, she sat in the gallery especially reserved for the Queen. " To the wife's place in the chapel of Versailles she felt she had a right; there with a quiet conscience and a tranquil heart she might kneel in the presence of her God."

The Church was delighted with the marriage which was the security of its influence. " You have an excellent partner, Sire," said the Bishop of Chartres to King Louis, " full of discernment and of

the Spirit of God, whose tenderness, fidelity and
affection for you are unequalled."

The most important event in the latter half of the
reign of Louis XIV was the Revocation of the Edict
of Nantes, which delegalised the Reformed religion
and sent shiploads of Huguenot refugees to England, greatly to England's commercial advantage.
Michelet holds Mme. de Maintenon responsible for
the Revocation, but Louis XIV believed, as Elizabeth had believed before him, that one religion was
quite enough for one nation. As a Catholic he
properly desired that his people should be Catholic.
As a sovereign he properly desired that his people
should not be divided in religious allegiance. The
quarrels between Catholics and Huguenots had
been a disturbing factor in the history of France for
generations, and it was reasonable, if short-sighted,
statesmanship to attempt the suppression of Protestantism altogether. To the King the terms
heresy and rebellion were synonymous. Any-
way, it was the King and not his wife who was
responsible for the abandonment of the policy of
Liberalism initiated by Henry IV. As a matter of
fact, Mme. de Maintenon never lost her admiration
for Huguenot pride and Huguenot Puritanism.
She was, as has been well said, a Protestant living
within the Catholic Church, and it is characteristic

that the Sacred Office that she loved best was not
the Mass, but Vespers with its chanting of the
Psalms.

The Revocation of the Edict of Nantes was
largely political. It was also popular. The great
majority of the French people remained faithful to
the old religion, and a new, fervent and intensely
national life had come to the Church at the end of
the seventeenth century thanks to the influence of
Bossuet, who had converted Turenne to Catholicism, Bourdaloue, and a host of other gifted ecclesiastics who taught that Catholics themselves must
first be converted before the Huguenots could be
drawn back to the fold.

In her later years, Mme. de Maintenon effected
her great achievement of establishing a school for
the education of gentlewomen in the Catholic faith
at Saint-Cyr, now and since the Revolution the
Sandhurst of France. Saint-Cyr became the great
preoccupation of de Maintenon's life. It was not
to be a convent in the ordinary sense. With her
Protestant upbringing she was impatient of what
she called " the silliness of nuns." Saint-Cyr was
a school, not a seminary. She enlisted the help of
the most gifted of her friends, of Racine, who wrote
a play especially for the young ladies to perform, of
Fénelon, of Bossuet. But she had to face all sorts

of trouble and anxieties mainly caused by the celebrated Mme. de Guyon, whose doctrine of Quietism
was denounced by the Church. The subsequent
trouble with Rome caused almost the only disa-
greement that ever occurred between de Maintenon
and the King.

She continued on excellent terms with the King's
children—he had ten living children, legitimate and
illegitimate—and with his grandchildren. Her influence over him continued. Versailles remained
sober and dull. The King never failed in his
religious duties, but he was often weary and bored,
and de Maintenon, as she grew older, grew bored
too.

Tragedy haunted the King's last days. The
glory of his reign was dissipated in the disasters of
the wars of the early years of the eighteenth century
which concluded with the Peace of Utrecht, and
the internal peace of his kingdom was disturbed
by the religious quarrels between the Jesuits and
Jansenists.

Louis died in 1715 at the age of seventy-seven.
On his deathbed he sent for his great-grandson, the
future Louis XV, and gave him wise counsel.
" Never forget what you owe to God. Do not
imitate me by making war. Try to keep the peace
with your neighbours, to comfort your people as far

as possible." Alas that such wise words should have fallen on such deaf ears! To de Maintenon he said: "I thought it would be harder to die than this. I assure you it is not a very terrible business; it does not seem to me to be difficult at all." He told her that he was sorry that he had not made her happy, but he assured her that he had always loved and esteemed her, and it was characteristic of her that she urged him not to give a thought to anyone but God.

After his death, Mme. de Maintenon quietly retired to Saint-Cyr, where she lived for another three years in complete retirement. Her biographer says:

"She slipped completely out of sight, shut herself up. Her women cut the stitches that held the gold embroideries on her skirts. She gave away her linen, her flowered muslin gowns, would keep nothing but her silver-plate, her gold spoon and fork, her wearing apparel. She dismissed her servants, keeping only two waiting-women, and a lackey to do her commissions out of doors; sold her coach, set to work at once, with characteristic quiet and practical diligence, to draw up the lists of her pensions, and her charitable gifts to enable certain unmarried ladies to live outside the convent, and to her poor."

The rest that she had longed for had come to her. In her last years at Versailles, her life had become almost unendurable. From half-past seven in the morning until late at night she had been at the King's beck and call with hardly a moment for meditation and prayer. But she had carried through the mission to which she had set herself. The task had been no easy one, and in these last years at Saint-Cyr peace and content came to her for the first time. She died in her sleep on April 16th, 1717, having, when she knew her death was certain, paid all her pensions in advance so that none of her dependents should suffer.

In January, 1794, after the Revolution, workmen busy with the destruction of the chapel at Saint-Cyr discovered a coffin in which they found the body of Mme. de Maintenon, fully dressed and perfectly preserved. With revolutionary fervour they took the corpse from the coffin, stripped it, and cast it into a hole in the common graveyard.

De Maintenon completely fulfilled the mission to which she had set her hand—the conversion of a King—and the man first enthralled by the gentle Louise de la Vallière and afterwards indifferent to her pain and suffering, then held in thrall by the strumpet de Montespan, was for over thirty years held by her quiet persistence and for twenty-two years was her faithful, if sometimes resentful, husband.

M. Paul Bourget has summed up the character of this very great lady. She was, he says, " upright, austere, faithful and true."

NELL GWYNNE

O N a March morning in the year 1671, Mr. John Evelyn, taking a walk through St. James's Park, was sadly shocked. In 1671, Evelyn was a staid civil servant in his early fifties, occupying much the same official position as that recently adorned by Mr. George Lansbury. It was part of his business to care for the parks of His Majesty King Charles II, and the improvement of his streets, and in St. James's Park he was particularly interested in the trees of which he had a considerable knowledge. Mr. John Evelyn was a good Churchman and a conscientious man, but something of a Puritan, and not a little pompous. "A most excellent person he is," said his friend Mr. Samuel Pepys, "and must be allowed a little for a little conceitedness."

On this spring morning Evelyn was distracted from his trees. A very pretty woman, with twinkling eyes and a jolly laugh, was sitting on the top of the wall which separated the garden of her house in Pall Mall from the Park, the King himself was joking and gossiping to her, and Evelyn could not help overhearing the " very familiar discourse." The woman was Nell Gwynne, " Sweet Nell of Old Drury," who had captured the hearts of all London when she was seventeen by her genius as a comic actress, and who now, at the age of twenty-one, was established as one of the King's favourites.

It is not quite established where Nell was born. Hereford claims to be her birthplace and so does Oxford. But in all probability she first saw the light in an alley off Drury Lane, then called Coal Yard and afterwards renamed Goldsmith Street. In any case it is certain that while she was quite a baby her family was living in this squalid neighbourhood. Her father was a Welsh soldier who was ruined in the Civil War. Her mother was a confirmed and utterly immoral drunkard. Her elder sister, Rose, was married to a highwayman and was herself imprisoned in Newgate when Nell was thirteen. Her father had apparently become a seventeenth-century costermonger, hawking vegetables in the streets. Mr. Dasent, Nell's biographer, quotes a satire of the time in which Nell is made to say:

> You that have seen me in my youthful age
> Preferred from stall of turnips to the stage.

While she was quite a child, Nell herself hawked herrings and oysters and was the bullied servant of a disreputable old hag in a house in another of the Drury Lane alleys where, generations later, Jonathan Wild lived and Jack Sheppard was arrested.

Then, as now, the theatre was the dominating interest of Drury Lane. During the Commonwealth the performance of stage plays had been sternly forbidden, but immediately after the Restoration the theatre became both the fashionable and the popular amusement, the King being its chief patron. Licences were given to Killigrew and Davenant to build theatres in London. The King's Theatre in Drury Lane was opened under the management of Killigrew in 1663, and Nell, pretty, intelligent, world-experienced in her early teens, was among the girls permitted to sell oranges in the theatre, a pleasanter occupation than selling herrings in the street.

Killigrew was a theatrical revolutionary. Until his time the women's parts in plays had been acted by boys and men, and there is a story that King Charles was once kept waiting for a performance of *Hamlet* to begin until the "Queen" had been shaved ! The first actress to appear in Killigrew's theatre, and therefore the first actress ever seen in

England, was probably Nan Marshall, the daughter of a Presbyterian minister who would certainly have hotly denounced the theatre and all its works. Killigrew established a school for young players. He was attracted by the pretty, impudent orange girl, " a bold, merry slut," as Pepys called her, and Nell became one of the pupils, being taught to act and dance by one Charles Hart, who was a great-nephew of Shakespeare. Evelyn, by the way, strongly disapproved of the new fashion. He records in his *Diary* that " foul and indecent women are now (and never till now) permitted to appear and act."

Nell made her first appearance in the spring of 1665. Her first conspicuous success was in Dryden's *The Indian Emperor*, and the King was present at the first night. The part could hardly have suited her. All her subsequent successes were made in comedy, and writing two years later of her performance in Dryden's play, Pepys says: " Nell's ill-speaking of a great part made me mad." Nell herself agreed with Pepys. She knew quite well that she could not play tragedy. In an epilogue which she spoke to the play *The Duke of Lerma*, she said:

> I know you in your hearts
> Hate serious plays—as I hate serious parts.

But, however well or badly she acted, the girl was a success from the beginning. A few weeks afterwards Pepys records at another performance: " Pretty, witty Nell sat next to us, which pleased me mightily." Killigrew soon discovered her comedy genius, and in 1667, writing of a performance of Dryden's *The Maiden Queen*, Pepys said:

" There is a comical part done by Nell, which is Florimell, that I never can hope ever to see the like done again, by man or woman. The King and Duke of York were at the play. But so great performance of a comical part was never I believe in the world before as Nell do this, both as a mad girlie, then most and best of all when she comes in like a young gallant; and hath the motions and carriage of a spark the most that ever I saw any man have. It makes me, I confess, admire her."

In the last act, Nell brought down the house by dancing a jig, dressed as a boy. " Nell in her boy's clothes," says Pepys, " mighty pretty."

Brought up as she was, and living in the dissolute atmosphere of the Restoration theatre, it was not to be supposed that she could be much affected by moral scruples. In 1667, two years after her debut, she spent a summer holiday at Epsom with Lord Buckhurst. The rakes of the Restoration were not without their pretty accomplishments. Among

the party at Epsom was Charles Sedley, who
wrote the delightful song—

> Phillis is my only joy,
> Faithless as the winds or seas,
> Sometimes cunning, sometimes coy,
> Yet she never fails to please;

and Buckhurst himself was the author of graceful
verse. This summer at Epsom was Nell's introduction into polite and raffish society. She soon,
however, quarrelled with Buckhurst and was back
again in the theatre at the end of August. She was
now seventeen, a girl of middle height with bronze
red hair, sapphire blue eyes, two rows of perfect
teeth, a marvellous complexion and a saucily tilted
nose. She was introduced to the King early in
1668, and she supped with him and his brother
the Duke of York, mightily amusing Charles by her
pretty impudence.

Nell appears to have acted for the last time in the
early days of 1670. When she was established as
an actress, she took a lodging at the Strand end of
Drury Lane, which was then as fashionable as the
other end was sordid. From her window she
could see the famous Maypole re-erected in the
Strand at the Restoration, where on one May Day,
on his way from the city, Pepys saw " many milk-
maids with their garlands upon their pails, dancing

with a fiddler before them." When she left Drury
Lane, she was installed by the King in an apart-
ment in Lincoln's Inn Fields, and there her first
son, afterwards the Duke of St. Albans, was
born. The boy was made Hereditary Master
Falconer and Hereditary Registrar of the Court
of Chancery, two well-paid sinecures that remained
in his family until recent times. In 1671, Nell
moved to the house in Pall Mall where she lived
until her death. She was then twenty-one, and it
had only taken her four years to " arrive." It is
curious how little the gay life of the Court and the
theatre appears to have been affected by the
grievous troubles of the times. In 1665, London
suffered from the plague. In 1666 came the Great
Fire, and in the next year a Dutch fleet sailed up the
Thames and destroyed the English ships anchored
at the mouth of the Medway. Nell Gwynne and
her friends seem to have cared for none of these
things.

Prosperity did not spoil Nell in the least. She
remained good-hearted, affectionate, irresponsible.
She even took her drunken old mother to live with
her in her Pall Mall house, and among her household bills, discovered a few years ago, was a
chemist's account for " plasters, glysters and cor-
dials " for Mrs. Gwynne. Her mother, however,

was incorrigible, and a lodging had to be found for her in Pimlico, where she fell into a ditch and was drowned in 1679. Rochester wrote of her:

> Nor was the mother's funeral less her care,
> No cost, no velvet, did the daughter spare;
> Fine gilded 'scutcheons did the Herse enrich,
> To celebrate this Martyr of the Ditch.

Nell was not in the least avaricious, never receiving anything like the money that was showered on the King's other mistresses and particularly on the Frenchwoman, Louise de Querouaille, afterwards Duchess of Portsmouth, who was loathed by the people of London as much as Nell was loved. But though her greed was never excessive, the ex-orange girl had the income of a great lady. She had her coach-and-four and her own sedan-chair. Her pearl necklace cost £4,000, and she could lose £1,400 in an evening's gambling without serious inconvenience.

In 1675, such was the gross manner of the Court —in this as in many other things Charles followed the example of Louis XIV—Nell was installed as one of the Queen's ladies-in-waiting, and had her right of entry into the Palace of Whitehall, a long straggling series of buildings that filled the space between the present Whitehall and the river, and which in addition to the royal apartments housed a

motley crew of courtiers and hangers-on. One of
the Palace's river gates was almost exactly where
the National Liberal Club now stands. There is a
certain irony in recalling the fact that Charles must
have often handed Sweet Nell of Old Drury out of
her private barge on the spot where earnest Liberal
politicians now hurry to their lunch.

The Court lady was still "a bold, merry slut,"
laughing and chaffing and making fun of everyone.
She shared the popular dislike for Louise de Querouaille, whom she christened "Squinta Bella" on
account of the lady's squint, and the "Weeping
Willow" because of her habit of dissolving into
tears when her royal lover refused any of her im-
portunate demands. Louise sometimes replied in
kind. To a woman who had praised Nell's wit
and beauty she said: "Yes, Madam, but anybody
may know she has been an orange wench by her
swearing."

Nell must have been a strange and attractive
figure in the Whitehall of intrigue, plots, boredom
and lust without love. The English *gamine* was as
immoral as the French and English great ladies,
but she was infinitely more human, infinitely more
amusing, infinitely more kind-hearted. She knew
nothing about politics, but she was always eager
to be of help in time of trouble. When the Duke of

Buckingham was imprisoned in the Tower, it was Nell Gwynne who begged his release. Buckingham was perhaps the most evil of the evil men who surrounded Charles. He was utterly dissolute, but for political purposes was a patron of the Anabaptists. He made friends with " the debauchees by drinking with them, the sober by grave and serious discourse, the pious by going to Communion."

It was in Nell's rooms, too, that Monmouth, the King's unfortunate son, would take refuge when he was out of favour. She was never failing in kindness.

Evelyn has left a rather pompous but sufficiently accurate sketch of Charles II, written after the King's death. He says:

" He was a prince of many virtues and many gross imperfections; debonair, easy of access, not bloody nor cruel; his countenance fierce, his voice great, proper of person, every motion became him; a lover of the sea, and skilful in shipping; not affecting other studies, yet he had a laboratory, and knew of many empirical medicines and the easier mechanical mathematics; he loved painting and building, and brought in a politer way of living, which passed to luxury and intolerable expense. He had a particular talent in telling a story and facetious passages, of which he had innumerable; this made some buffoons and vicious wretches too presumptuous and familiar, not worthy the favour they abused. . . . He would doubtless have been an excellent prince had he been less addicted to women, who made him uneasy, and always in want to supply their unmeasurable profusion, to the detriment of many indigent persons who had signally served both him and his father. He frequently and easily changed favourites to his great prejudice."

Evelyn was a stubborn royalist determined to see the best in a King. There is, however, a consensus of contemporary opinion as to Charles's good temper, amiability and approachableness. De Grammont says:

" The King was inferior to none either in shape or air; his wit was pleasant; his disposition easy and affable; his soul, susceptible of opposite impressions, was compassionate to the unhappy, inflexible to the wicked, and tender even to excess; he showed great abilities in urgent affairs, but was incapable of application to any that were not so; his heart was often the dupe, but oftener the slave, of his engagements."

Charles was a tall man, some six feet in height, " well made, with a swarthy complexion agreeing well with his fine black eyes, a large ugly mouth, a graceful and dignified carriage, and a fine figure."

A by no means flattering comparison may be made between the characters of the English Charles II and his cousin the French Louis XIV. Louis XIV had a grandiose conception of his high office. He was the vicegerent of God. While his love of his country was in effect love of himself, it was a dignified passion. It made him as eager to make the Gallican Church independent of Rome, so far as that was possible, as he was to make France the dominant state in Europe. The French King's profligacy was as notorious as the English King's. But his mistresses were selected with some discretion and were always women of good birth. To Louis, kingship meant power. To Charles, kingship meant idleness with plenty of money to spend. He had had his years of exile and bitter poverty. He had been shrewd enough to realise that if he had listened to his mother's pleading and joined the Roman Church, he would never have recovered his father's crown. He had returned to England at the Restoration to find himself, probably much to his surprise, a national hero. "All the world is in a merry mood because of the King's coming," wrote Pepys, and Evelyn describes the scene in London when the King made his entrance, "the ways

strewed with flowers, the bells ringing, the streets
hung with tapestry, fountains running with wine."
Evelyn adds: " Such a restoration was never mentioned in any history ancient or modern since the
return of the Jews from the Babylonish captivity."

Back again in London, Charles was determined
to have a good time according to his own lights.
To a large extent he was disappointed. His reign
was one long series of political complications, which
were infinitely tiresome to a quite extraordinarily
lazy man. He was not without political shrewdness. Partly, though not entirely, from goodwill
to the Roman Catholics, he favoured religious toler-
ation, but his Parliaments, swayed by Anglican
squirearchy, were all for intolerance.

He was anxious to reconcile the English Church
to Rome, on conditions that would have insured
her a considerable measure of independence. But
the exaggerated anti-Papalism of his Parliament
encouraged and made possible the rascalities of
Titus Oates and his associates. Bored by the
futility of politicians, he escaped to his mistresses.

And always he needed money, and in order to
secure the money necessary to bribe corrupt politicians and to pay for the extravagances of his
ladies, he sold England to France. The intention
of Louis in signing the notorious secret treaty was

that England should become permanently subject to the Bourbon monarchy, and that might actually have happened had not the war with Holland proved much more costly than was anticipated. In consequence Charles made demands that Louis could not fulfil, and the English King was compelled again to submit his policy to Parliament.

The King's principal preoccupation was his health. He played games regularly and rather well, and always at the end of a game of tennis he had himself weighed so that he might know exactly the effect that the exercise had on him. It was this devotion to exercise that enabled him to endure "the uncontrolled debauchery of thirty years." No historical personage has ever had the harem habit so thoroughly as the second Charles. His latest biographer, Mr. Arthur Bryant, says: " His extreme susceptibility where women were concerned was the Achilles heel of his armour; through that gap every arrow could pierce." Halifax was blunter. He said: " His inclinations to love were the effects of health and a good constitution with as little mixture of the seraphic as ever man had. I am apt to think his stayed as much as any man's ever did in the lower region."

After the Restoration, Lady Castlemaine was the mistress *en titre*. Barbara Villiers, Countess of

Castlemaine, had known Charles during his exile in
Holland and had returned with him to England.
She was created Duchess of Cleveland in 1670, and
she was the mother of three sons, each of whom
became a duke—the Duke of Southampton, the
Duke of Grafton, and the Duke of Northumberland.
Bishop Burnet says of her: " She was a woman of
great beauty, most enormously vicious and raven-
ous, foolish but imperious, very uneasy to the King
and always carrying on intrigues with other men
while yet she pretended she was jealous of him."
Charles seems to have put up with her tantrums
with the utmost amiability. De Grammont describes one typical scene between them:

" The impetuosity of her temper broke forth like
lightning. She told him, ' that it very ill became
him to throw out such reproaches against one who,
of all the women in England, deserved them the
least; that he had never ceased quarrelling thus
unjustly with her, ever since he had betrayed his
own mean low inclinations; that to gratify such a
depraved taste as his, he wanted only such silly
things as Stewart, Wells, and that pitiful strolling
actress, whom he had lately introduced into their
society.' Floods of tears, from rage, generally
attended these storms; after which, resuming the
part of Medea, the scene closed with menaces of

tearing her children in pieces, and setting his palace on fire. What course could he pursue with such an outrageous fury, who, beautiful as she was, resembled Medea less than her dragons, when she was thus enraged ?"

After Castlemaine came the French Louise de Querouaille, afterwards Duchess of Portsmouth, whom Nell bitterly hated and always candidly described in the argot of Drury Lane. She had been a lady-in-waiting to Charles's fascinating sister, Henriette of England, the first wife of the French King's brother, whom Charles loved more than he ever loved any other man or woman, and had been sent to England as a French agent to attract the fancy of the King and to secure the treaty to which I have referred. Evelyn says that " she had, in my opinion, a childish, simple and baby face."

The greatest beauty of the Court of Whitehall and the woman of all women with whom Charles was most in love, perhaps because she did not fall into his lap, was Frances Louisa Stewart, afterwards Duchess of Richmond. " With her hat cocked and a red plume, with her sweet eye, little Roman nose and excellent taille she is now the greatest beauty I ever saw in my life," said Pepys. And de Grammont says:

" She was childish in her behaviour, and laughed

at everything, and her taste for frivolous amusements, though unaffected, was only allowable in
girls about twelve or thirteen years old. A child,
however, she was, in every other respect except
playing with a doll; blind-man's buff was her
most favourite amusement; she was building
castles of cards, while the deepest play was going on
in her apartments, where you saw her surrounded
by eager courtiers, who handed her the cards, or
young architects, who endeavoured to imitate her."

This was Whitehall. There was little there of
the elaborate ceremonial etiquette of Versailles in
the early part of the reign of Louis XIV, and certainly none of the decorous gloom created through
the influence of Mme. de Maintenon. But everything was done in public. There were no secrets
in Whitehall, and there was no privacy. Pepys
records:

" By and by the King to dinner, and I waited
there his dining; but Lord! how little I should be
pleased, I think, to have so many people crowding
about me; and among other things it astonished me
to see my Lord Berkshire waiting at table and
serving the King drink, in that dirty pickle as I
never saw man in my life."

The immoralities of Versailles were denounced
by the Church. Great preachers like Bossuet

chided Louis in public, and urged him to repentance, and at the end of his reign there was a
religious revival in France that affected the life
of the royal palace, if, indeed, it did not begin there.
But the Church was silent in England. Dissenting
preachers denounced the King, the people sometimes resented his naughtinesses. But there was no
English Bossuet, though there was one notable
exception to the general acceptance of the doctrine
that the King could do no wrong. In 1684, Nell
Gwynne went to Winchester with Charles, and the
saintly Ken, then one of the Canons, refused to
allow her to lodge in his house. Neither Nell nor
Charles ever bore any malice, and when shortly
afterwards Ken's name was mentioned for a
bishopric, the King said: "Who should have Bath
and Wells but the little black fellow who would
not give poor Nelly a night's lodging?"

On the other hand, two years earlier, on her
way back with Charles from the Newmarket races,
Nell was entertained by the Vice-Chancellor of
Cambridge University, of course a clergyman, who
presented her with an address of welcome in verse.
Oxford was not so friendly. Soon after she was
mobbed at Oxford, the people thinking that she
was the unpopular Duchess of Portsmouth. It
was on this occasion that she put her head out of

the coach window and said: "Pray, good people, be civil; I am the Protestant mistress."

The pleasantest achievement of Nell Gwynne's life was the foundation of Chelsea Hospital for disabled soldiers. It was she to whom the idea first occurred. It was she who insisted that Wren's plans should be altered and that the Hospital should be made much larger, and she was with the King when the foundation stone was laid in 1682. A long list could be made of her kindnesses—a generous subscription towards the relief of unfortunates rendered homeless by fire, payment of the debt of a clergyman arrested by his creditors, and so on. After the King's death, and when she herself was hard pressed for money, she saved from starvation the poet Otway, who had been the tutor of her eldest son.

Charles gave her a country house at Burford, near Windsor, and there Nell spent perhaps the happiest days of her life. She had a garden with an orangery, pleasure grounds and a bowling alley, and her children to play with. She had stabling for a hundred horses and forty-five coaches !

In 1685, on Nell's thirty-fifth birthday, Charles had an apoplectic seizure and died four days later at the age of fifty-four, having first been received into the Roman Catholic Church. On his deathbed, according to Evelyn, " he spake to the Duke (his brother) to be kind to the Duchess of Cleveland and especially Portsmouth and that Nelly should not starve."

Nelly did not starve, but most of the fun and the joy went out of her life with the death of her royal lover. England was a dreary place during the reign of King James II, with its political troubles, its Monmouth rebellion, its Judge Jeffreys and its Bloody Assize. Nell was often hard pressed for money—indeed, she was threatened with imprisonment for debt. In a petition to the King she said: " God knows I never loved your brother interestedly. Had he lived he told me before he died that the world should see by what he did for me that he had both love and value for me. He was my friend, and allowed me to tell him all my griefs, and did, like a friend, advise me and told me who was my friend and who was not."

James paid her debts, but she remained in financial low water until the end, and her jewels, including the famous £4,000 pearl necklace, had to be sold. She was taken ill in March, 1687, and died on November 14th. In her will everyone was remembered. No servant's name was forgotten, and something was left to her nurses. It is said that, following the example of her royal lover, Nell

Gwynne became a Roman Catholic before her death. Evelyn spitefully wrote in his *Diary* in 1686: " Dryden the famous play writer and his two sons and Mrs. Nelly were said to go to Mass. Such proselytes were no great loss to the Church." But, so far as Nell Gwynne is concerned, the story is not true.

She was buried in the church of St. Martin-in-the-Fields, and the Vicar, Dr. Tenison, afterwards Archbishop of Canterbury, preached the sermon. For this he was severely criticised. Queen Mary, the wife of William III, who had then ascended the throne, was his warm defender. " I have heard of the sermon," said the Queen, " and it is a sign that the poor unfortunate woman died penitent; for if I have read a man's heart through his looks, had she not made a truly pious end, the Doctor could never have been persuaded to speak well of her."

In her origin, Nell was the kin of Du Barry, the lowly born and intriguing successor of La Pompadour in the affections of Louis XV, of whom Carlyle, in a fine Presbyterian frenzy, wrote: " What a course was thine; from that first truckle bed (in Joan of Arc's country) where thy mother bore thee in tears to an unnamed father; forward through the lowest subterranean depths and over highest sunlit heights of Harlotdom and Rascaldom—to the guillotine axe, which shears away thy vainly whimpering head." Nell was luckier and, though similar in origin, infinitely different in character, proving, such are the ironies of human life, that a large measure of kindliness and a certain measure of joy are sometimes to be found in Harlotdom and Rascaldom.

IT is one of history's little ironies that it is due to the success with which Jeanne Antoinette, Marquise de Pompadour, amused Louis XV of France, *le roi fainéant*, the " King Do-nothing," and to the fact that, as a reward, she was allowed to meddle as she would with international politics that the sun never sets on the British flag. With the help of two other women, Elizabeth of Russia and Maria Theresa of Austria, Jeanne Antoinette ruined France and laid the foundations both of the British and the German Empires.

Jeanne Antoinette owed nothing of her eminence to her heredity. Her grandfather was a peasant. Her father had all the French peasant's shrewdness and none of his scruples. He was in the service of a firm of army contractors, and he did so well for himself that he was sentenced to be hanged, and only saved his life by a flight to Germany, finally obtaining a remission of the sentence through payment of four hundred thousand *livres*. Her mother was the utterly immoral daughter of a butcher.

But Madame Poisson was a very shrewd lady and, according to her lights—if lights they can be called —not a bad mother. Both her children, Jeanne Antoinette and her brother Abel, were strikingly handsome and excellently educated, and while she was still in her cradle Jeanne was intended by her mother for the King's favourite. It sounds very horrible, but Madame Poisson was little worse than the average mother of her era. The maternal ambition was stimulated by a fashionable fortune-teller who foretold that the child would be not a queen, but " almost a queen." So after a short time in an Ursuline convent, Jeanne Antoinette was carefully taught all the accomplishments calculated to attract the *blasé* and the semi-cultured, for the Paris of Louis XV was as enthusiastic for easily acquired superficial culture as the New York of 1931.

No pains were spared to make Jeanne Antoinette, Marcelle Tinayre says, " an epitome of all the feminine graces and all the feminine accomplishments." She was taught to sing and dance and sketch and play the harpsichord. The result was a highly intelligent girl, quite unmoral, but genuinely interested in art and letters. She was " very ill born and very well educated."

Her girlhood was lived at the beginning of the

age of the philosophers, which was the prelude to the Revolution, and Jeanne's mother had money enough and " push " enough to be regularly invited into the decent middle-class society, frequented by lawyers and prosperous traders, where the new philosophy was discussed, and where, indeed, the Revolution was prepared.

When she was twenty, Jeanne Antoinette married a comparatively wealthy and well-connected young man, Le Normand d'Etiolles, and with some little difficulty, for her mother's reputation was notorious, she collected at her house in Paris and her country house at Etiolles a pleasant circle of intellectual friends, the most famous of whom was Voltaire, then a man of nearly fifty, whose play *Mahomet*, recently produced in Paris, had given him the beginning of his popular fame. As a boy, Voltaire had received small favours from Ninon de l'Enclos. As a man, he was to be considerably indebted to another of the same sisterhood.

The young Mme. d'Etiolles was extraordinarily attractive. She was a blonde with an exquisite complexion and regular features. Marcelle Tinayre thus describes her:

" Her features were regular and delicate. The lips, a little too pale, but bitten into colour by the pretty teeth, could smile enchantingly; the brow

was made to have the hair thus drawn straight
back, then lifted in soft waves obedient to the head's
pure line—that chestnut hair on which the powder
spread its silver, but was powerless to hide the gold.
The eyebrows were two fair, unbroken arches; and
in the eyes, whose hue was ever changing—were
they blue or green or brown?—the light of intelligence gleamed radiant. Lissom was the form, and
ravishing were the arms and hands; the rounded
neck sufficed to ' fill a manly hand '—and all this
charming personality in its spreading skirts of puffed
brocade, its ribboned bodices afroth with lace, its
dainty slippers, with its little knot of flowers on
shoulder or on bosom, seemed (said a contemporary) to ' draw the line between the last degree of
elegance and the first of aristocracy.' "

And a woman who hated her said: " There was
in her countenance a most attractive blending of
vivacity and tenderness, and a delightful gift of
badinage, piquant but refined, gave an unusual
interest to her conversation."

Temperamentally Jeanne Antoinette was cold
and calculating. She was an affectionate enough
mother and, in the circumstances, a wonderfully
good daughter, but her success in the career chosen
for her was due not a little to the fact that never
in her life did she know anything of passion. Her

husband adored her, but she was quite determined
to be unfaithful to him, though with no one less
exalted than the King. That was the ambition
that her mother had instilled into her, and she
waited with growing impatience and angled with
infinite skill.

The Regency that followed the death of Louis
XIV had come to an end in 1723, and the dead
King's great-grandson, Louis XV, began his reign.
Louis was good-looking, lazy, indifferent, often
drunk, unspeakably vicious, a Charles II without
his charm and without his shrewdness. He was
brutal, morbid, and almost inconceivably ill-
mannered, secretive, and a master of dissimulation.
M. Louis Ducros says in his *French Society in the
Eighteenth Century*:

"Some of the subjects which he took most
pleasure in discussing were of an embarrassing
nature. 'The details of illnesses and operations
and questions as to the place of one's prospective
burial are, unfortunately, his usual queries.' It
should be added that it amused him to address these
to the sick and old, which enhanced their polite-
ness. He was often cruel in his talk, and, apparently, without suspecting it. At the *Lever du Roi*,
M. de Fontanieu's nose had bled, upon which the
King said to him: 'Take care; at your age that is

the forerunner of an apoplectic stroke.' Another day, when dining in public, the King having asked for news of one of his intimates, was informed that he was dead. ' Well, I warned him of it,' said he, and then, turning to the courtiers who surrounded him, and fixing the Abbé de Broglie with his eye, he addressed him with these words, ' Your turn next.' "

The Queen, Marie Leczinska, a Polish princess, was pious, kindly, greedy and unattractive. "The Queen," said Talleyrand, " was venerated, but her virtues were of rather a gloomy nature and never stirred any enthusiasm on her behalf. She lacked the beauty which made the nation so proud of Louis XV's good looks."

The Queen was the mother of many dull children, and her four daughters lived to play their pitiful part in the drama of the Revolution. Rag, Snif, Pig and Dud their unpleasant father called them.

In 1744, Louis was taken dangerously ill at Metz and very nearly died. His recovery brought him a short burst of popularity. He was still young and he was good-looking, and, for a few months, he was to all France " Louis the Well-Beloved." When he actually died, thirty years later, he was to all France " Louis the Well-Hated." All that he asked of life was to be amused, and the nation paid dearly for the amusement. France starved while its King fiddled, and, while Versailles was filled with extravagant futilities, "lank scarecrows prowled hunger-stricken through all the highways and byways of French existence."

Twenty-four-year-old Jeanne Antoinette thought of none of these things as she angled for Louis. He was the King. What did it matter what sort of king he was?

In December, 1744, the royal mistress of the moment died, and the King was looking about him. He had his corps of spies, whose business it was to discover beautiful women outside the Court circle of Versailles, and from one of them he heard of the charm of the lady whom he had casually noticed watching, with others of the Paris middle class, the royal hunts in the forest of Senart.

In her *Madame-Geoffrin, Her Salon and her Times,* Janet Aldis says:

" Her fair brilliant complexion never looked more fair and brilliant than when, in a long riding-dress of rich blue velvet, ornamented with embossed gold buttons, with a felt hat of the same colour, from which floated a waving white plume, she rode along the forest paths, excited at the thought of the possibility of meeting his Majesty."

Jeanne Antoinette first actually met the King at

a masked ball given at Versailles to celebrate the marriage of the Dauphin in February, 1745. They met again, a few days afterwards, at another ball, given by the citizens of Paris at the Hôtel de Ville, when there was a horrible crush and " the refreshments gave out three hours after midnight," and before Easter she was the acknowledged *maîtresse en titre*.

Her husband, be it said to his credit, implored, protested, threatened suicide, and was finally exiled. And Jeanne Antoinette was amused. She was always the Woman Without a Heart. But while she was indifferent to her husband and to all other men as lovers, she was never forgetful of her friends. Almost the first favour that she asked of Louis was the appointment of Voltaire as " historiographer of France."

1745 was a golden year for Jeanne Antoinette. In the summer, Marshal Saxe's victory over the English, the Austrians and the Dutch at Fontenoy —a useless enough victory as it was to prove— suggested that her coming to Versailles was the prelude to the recovery of the military glory of the last reign. Voltaire wrote verses in her praise. The Abbé Bernis, whom she was to make one of the King's ministers, sang songs about her dimples to the accompaniment of his lute, and in the autumn she was created the Marquise de Pompadour and was formally presented to the Queen. It was no new thing at the Court of Versailles for a Queen to be compelled to receive her husband's favourites. A generation before, Louise de la Vallière, blushing and ashamed, had curtsied to " the chubby fat little consort " of Louis XIV, and, for some queer reason, the pious Polish Marie found it easier to endure the new middle-class mistress than she had found it to receive the Court ladies whom she had succeeded. Jeane Antoinette, too, was clever enough always to show proper deference to the Queen. She was too clever to be rude. The Dauphin was less courteous than his mother. When Jeanne Antoinette was presented to him, he put out his tongue at her and, as a punishment, was packed off to Meudon in disgrace.

The Court at Versailles in the reign of Louis XV was a centre of hypocrisy and demoralisation. Great nobles were implicated in swindles. Despite the fact that they were living in the age of philosophers, the courtiers were almost incredibly uneducated and ignorant. As Montesquieu said: " No one can compete with the ignorance of those who frequent the Court of France." Manners were coarse, drunkenness was habitual and, indeed, eating and drinking appear to have been the

most popular of the Versailles amusements. It
is almost incredible how much the French royal
family and the courtiers are said to have
managed to eat. The Queen's dinners always
consisted of twenty-nine courses, and the royal
princesses, the pathetic Rag, Snif, Pig and Dud,
used to lock themselves into their apartments and
eat all day long. The courtiers played cards and
habitually cheated, and petty pilfering was the
rule in the great ramshackle palace. But the
King was regular in his attendance at church and
fervent in his prayers, and when she was established at Versailles, La Pompadour heard Mass
every day, which suggested to the witty Mme.
de Sévigné that the favourite "belonged neither
to God nor to the devil."

La Pompadour had her apartments in Versailles,
none too comfortable from this century's point of
view, next to the King's. She had arrived at the
height of her ambition, but she soon found the
constant company of the insatiable royal amorist
infinitely wearisome. To him she was a dis-
appointing "cold sea bird," and she realised that
it was going to be a tremendous task to hold her
place. "This upstart of genius," to use Marcelle
Tinayre's striking phrase, strained every nerve to
be amusing. She sang to the King. She never

ceased to be high-spirited and gay. She endured
his fits of black depression. Never did woman
play her card more cleverly. Quite naturally she
had to reckon with a legion of enemies—the
Dauphin and the Catholic party, who dreaded and
feared the philosophers whom she patronised, the
women who were her rivals, and soon the ministers
whom she caused to be dismissed. But she was
little afraid of their enmity, and probably amused.
It made life worth living in the deadly dull Palace
of Versailles.

Versailles was the home of an immoral roman-
ticism. King and courtiers fiddled rather badly on
fiddles out of tune while France was in travail and
the way was being prepared for the Revolution.
"While," says Janet Aldis, "famine was sweeping
like a death-blast through the provinces, while the
Archbishop of Tours was selling his silver plate to
save the poor of his diocese from death by starvation, she (La Pompadour) and the Court were
anxiously subscribing one hundred thousand *livres*
as an inducement to Jeliote, the celebrated singer,
to stay among them." La Pompadour was bored
by the futilities of the Court, bored by the kisses
of her lover. She was a clever woman, and politics
were her distraction. Louis was infinitely lazy,
and in a very short time it was she, and not the

King, who decided policy and shaped the destiny of France. To understand what she attempted and how completely she failed it is necessary to recall the conditions in Europe at the middle of the eighteenth century.

Frederick the Great, " the painted pervert of Potsdam," was King of Prussia, determined to make himself master of all Germany. Maria Theresa was Archduchess of Austria and Queen of Hungary and Bohemia, a woman of character and courage, equally determined to preserve her inheritance from Prussian aggression. George II—" dapper little George with his red face and his white eyebrows and goggle eyes," as Thackeray has described him —reigned in England, a German of the Germans, intent, for the most part, on curbing the power of France. The Bourbons and the Hapsburgs were hereditary enemies, and, consequently, Maria Theresa was inclined to alliance with England; but the England of the Georges, like the England of Victoria, was pro-Prussian, and, on the advice of the Empress Elizabeth of Russia, the daughter of Peter the Great, who hated Frederick the Great and the Prussians as much as Maria Theresa hated them, she determined to ally herself with France.

It was no easy matter to turn France from the policy of the great Louis, but Maria Theresa,

virtuous wife and admirable mother, did it by
flattering La Pompadour at the very moment when
she was most ambitious for political power.   An
autograph letter was sent from Vienna to Jeanne
Antoinette as from one sovereign to another—
it was addressed, so it is said, to " ma cousine "
—suggesting the advantages to France of alliance with Austria, and Jeanne Antoinette was
won by flattery. The letter arrived at the luckiest
moment. La Pompadour considered herself seriously affronted by Frederick of Prussia. When
Voltaire arrived at Potsdam, he told the King that
Mme. de Pompadour desired to present her respects
to his Majesty, and Frederick bluntly replied, " Je
ne la connais pas."   And Jeanne Antoinette never
forgot.   Afterwards, in the fluctuating fortunes of
war, Frederick tried to buy her friendship, first
with a bribe of a hundred and twenty thousand
pounds, and afterwards with the Principality of
Neuchâtel.   But La Pompadour would not listen.
"I hate the man," she said.   "Let us pulverise
the Attila of the North."

The King was indifferent to the suggested change
of policy.   His ministers protested and were dismissed.   The Abbé Bernis, who had sung of the
favourite's dimples to his lute, was given high
office, and France was pledged to support Austria

in a war in which she had no direct interest and which was to destroy her European influence until it was restored by the victories of Napoleon. And all this happened because a pretty woman of thirty demanded to play the leading part in a game that she did not understand.

La Pompadour now actually reigned in the Palace of Versailles. It was she, and not the King, who nominated ministers and dictated policy. Cabinet councils were held in her room, and, through the Director of the Post Office, who was one of her creatures, letters were intercepted, and she thus had early knowledge of every intrigue launched against her and her policy. The Abbé Bernis was never more than a second-rate politician. When he failed her, she appointed Choiseul as Minister of Foreign Affairs. Choiseul had earned her favour by betraying his cousin, who had had an intrigue with the King. Before obtaining his place in the ministry, he had been appointed by La Pompadour French Ambassador in Rome and afterwards in Vienna, where he negotiated the treaty which was to cost France so dearly. Choiseul was a man of outstanding ability. It was impossible for him to save France from the misfortunes that followed the alliance with Austria, but he added San Domingo and Corsica to the French possessions, and, acting as the instrument of the woman to whom he owed his position, he patronised philosophers and persecuted the Jesuits, whom La Pompadour detested, but whose influence eventually wrought the minister's undoing. Choiseul remained France's chief minister until La Pompadour's death, and until his own death, four years before the Revolution, he was something of a popular hero.

La Pompadour was no ordinary king's mistress. She was " a great political force, she made and unmade ministers, she selected Ambassadors, she appointed generals, she confirmed pensions and places." And her influence was not wholly evil. It is to her that France owes the famous manufactory of Sèvres, as well as the establishment of the École Militaire. She was a great patron of arts and letters. Voltaire and Montesquieu owed much to her interest, she assisted Diderot and d'Alembert, and made the fame of Marmontel. She interested the King in the artists and sculptors of the day— drawing his especial attention to the works of Boucher and making him buy the artist's celebrated pictures, the *Lever du Soleil* and the *Coucher du Soleil*, now in the Wallace Collection.

The Pompadour foreign policy had its results in three great battles. In 1757, the Prussians defeated

the French and the Austrians at Rossbach, and
Prussia's predominance in Germany was assured.
In the same year, Clive won the battle of Plassey,
and it was decided that the English and not the
French should rule in India. And in 1759, the
heroic Montcalm was defeated by Wolfe at the
battle of the Heights of Abraham outside Quebec,
and Canada became part of the British Empire.
These misfortunes happened in La Pompadour's
lifetime. The crowning misfortune occurred after
her death, when Prussia and Austria made peace
and divided with Russia the territories of the kingdom of Poland, the constant friend of France.

There is no evidence whatever that La Pompadour realised the enormity of her blunder or that
she cared for the consequences a whit more than
Louis. Politics were her amusement. The holding of her place was her principal preoccupation.

The most dangerous of her enemies were the dismissed ministers, among them Maurepas, who
assailed her with the mocking verses, the *Poisson-
ades* (Poisson was her maiden name), that made
starving Paris laugh. Maurepas did not trouble to
mince his words. La Pompadour was a rogue and
a strumpet, whose soul was vile and mercenary, and
who had turned the French Court into a kennel not

fit for a dog.   Paris, as I say, laughed, but Maurepas
went into exile for twenty years.

La Pompadour's most effective device for amusing Louis was the institution of a company of
amateur actors, with an Abbé as prompter, who
performed Molière's *Tartuffe*, a dozen slight oper-
ettas, and Rousseau's *Le Devin de Village*, at the
first performance of which the author was present,
bashful, sulky, with an unkempt beard and un-
brushed wig.   The production was a great success,
and Rousseau was commanded next day to see the
King, but he refused to obey, thereby losing a comfortable pension.   He says in his *Confessions* :
" How should I afterwards have dared to speak
of disinterestedness and independence ?   Had I
received the pension, I must either have become a
flatterer or remained silent, and, moreover, who
would have insured to me the payment of it ?
What steps should I have been under the necessity
of taking ?   How many people must I have so-
licited ?   I should have had more trouble and
anxious cares in preserving than in doing without
it.   Therefore, I thought I acted according to my
principles by refusing, and sacrificing appearances
to reality."

The favourite had done her best to serve the
philosopher.   But philosophers are hard to serve.

13

La Pompadour was an old woman before she was forty. But life had its compensations. While France was starving, she had grown very rich. Her brother was a marquis with a profitable sinecure. She was the possessor of a dozen domains. She remained the friend of the philosophers, despite the fact that she was the chief beneficiary from the system that they attacked. But she was haunted by constant terror. He who had given could take away. She must retain the royal favour at any price. And far and away the greatest achievement of her life was to keep the King's intimate and confiding friendship when she had entirely lost his love, if love it can be called. That happened about six years after her installation at Versailles.

It is probably untrue that she herself acted as pander, and that she found girls for the disgusting orgies at the Parc aux Cerfs, the memory of which did more than anything else to insure the downfall of the Bourbon monarchy. But she took good care that no other woman of ability and character had any chance of influencing her ex-lover.

In 1754, La Pompadour's daughter, Alexandrine —her only child, and the daughter of her husband —died, and the mother, genuinely sorrow-stricken, and following from afar the example of La Vallière, had a fit of quite probably sincere religion. She

became more regular at her attendance at Mass.
She fasted every Friday.   She took a Jesuit as her
confessor.   The Queen rejoiced at her apparent
conversion.   The King thought it all very silly and
selected the occasion for nominating the Duchesse,
as she had now become, Lady-in-Waiting to his wife.
But Polish Maria vetoed the appointment of a lady
who did not live with her husband, and she was
backed by her honest Jesuit confessor.   There
followed a very ugly episode.   La Pompadour
wrote to her husband a blatantly insincere letter
in which she said:

" I am resolved, by my future conduct, to atone
for the errors of my past.   Take me back; you shall
find that to edify society by the united life I shall
lead with you as much as I may have scandalised
it by my separation from you, is the sole concern
of my days."

But d'Etiolles, who had loved her very dearly,
loved her no more, and he asked to be excused.
And the Jesuit made it so clear that he saw through
the humbug of the penitence that La Pompadour
became, as so many other worldlings have become
in similar circumstances, the bitter enemy of the
Order that, whatever may be its shortcomings, has
never been easily humbugged.

In 1757, an attempt was made on the King's life.

He was only very slightly wounded, but he was terrified, and in his nervous prostration, surrounded by his family and his chaplains, he never once asked for his favourite. This was taken by the Court as proof positive that her day was over. But she hung on for seven years longer, when she died of inflammation of the lungs.

She died at the age of forty-two in her apartments in the Château of Versailles. She knew she was dying, and she made a brave end. She had already received the consolations of religion, and the Curé of La Madeleine spent much time with her. On the morning of her death (April 15th, 1764) she read her will carefully over, charged her steward to recompense all who had attended her during her illness, and to give all the money in her desk to the poor. She then ordered her women to dress her, and put some colour on her pale cheeks. She gave an audience to Janette, the Intendant of the Post Office, reading and criticising the papers he submitted to her with her usual interest. The Curé then again came to her. When he was about to take his leave, the Marquise smiled and asked him to remain, saying: "One moment, Monsieur le Curé; we will take our departure together." A few moments later she died.

"My life has been a battle," said La Pompadour

on her deathbed. "She died fighting," says Sir Philip Gibbs, "and victorious to the last, against those Court factions which would have had her dragged at the cart's tail had she not been more subtle in intrigue, more powerful in crushing a half-developed plot, than these enemies were in concocting it. So La Pompadour passed, and with her the last shreds of dignity that still clothed the King."

Her body was hurried away from Versailles to the chapel of the Capuchins on the Place Vendôme where her daughter had been buried. It was raining hard, and Louis stood bareheaded on the balcony of his study watching the funeral procession in the evening gloom. But La Pompadour was soon forgotten, and the successor of the cultured friend of the philosophers was the gutter-snipe Du Barry.

The royal mistress was a serious factor in the life of the sixteenth, seventeenth and eighteenth centuries. She distributed favours. She was the source of political corruption and an active agent of mischief. But few royal mistresses have seriously affected the course of history. It would, for example, be merely absurd to hold Louise de Querouaille responsible for the betrayal of England to France by Charles II. La Pompadour, almost alone in her order, did actually play a controlling part in politics, and there is a certain moral satisfaction in the fact that no politician was ever a more complete failure. The truth is that, true to her type, she cared for nothing but herself and her fortune. She was as greedy as De Montespan and De Querouaille, though she was far more intelligent. But her intelligence was not very deep, and it must be remembered that it was the fashionable pose of the France of Louis XV.

La Pompadour wanted riches and position and adulation. She had them all. And France, beaten in battle and taxed to starvation, paid the bill. So did the Bourbons when the guillotine fell on the neck of La Pompadour's lover's grandson on the Place de la Révolution.

IT has often been said that his mother was Napoleon's best friend. In a sense, with the possible exception of Eugène Beauharnais, one or two of his personal servants, and (much more doubtfully) his sister Pauline, his mother was his only friend if a friend be he who is at least as ready to give as to receive. But the truth is that a Napoleon can have no friends. The climb in a few years from obscurity to supreme power is only possible to a ruthless and entirely egocentric personality, to whom friendship, with its tolerance, its give and take, its essential equality, is impossible. A Napoleon will buy and he will pay a sufficiently good price to make treachery unprofitable so long as he can go on paying. But he can receive nothing as a gift, for to him a gift is either an insult or the suggestion of betrayal. He must sit on his throne alone. At his zenith he is as inevitably alone as at his nadir—perhaps more alone. He may ask advice from his marshals and his counsellors. But he dare not admit their right to advise. That would be a practical abdication.

Napoleon was well served. Talleyrand was a master diplomat, and there is this to be said for the most famous turncoat in history, that he was faithful to his master until, with his acute capacity for reading the signs of the times, he realised that the Napoleonic drama had come to its final climax and that France was ruined unless Napoleon was banished. Fouché was a master spy, and no man is more necessary to a tyrant. Among the marshals were the most capable soldiers of a century. Napoleon successfully exploited the ability of his servants. Had they been his comrades, had he been content to be *primus inter pares*, the Empire might have continued, but it would not have been the Empire.

It is difficult for any man to silence the criticism of his family. It was quite impossible for a Corsican, for in Corsica the family was the clan to which ultimate allegiance was always given. When Napoleon rose, his family rose with him, hanging on to his coat tails, hampering, compromising, annoying. It is not true that his family contrived Napoleon's undoing. St. Helena was certain on the 18th Brumaire. But the family may have hastened the end, and they made it slightly ridiculous—

the well-meaning Joseph, an incompetent King
against his better judgment; the burlesque
Jerome, King of the impossible kingdom of
Westphalia; the treacherous Catherine. In the
days of glory, Joseph advised, Louis often protested, and Lucien, a man of character, courage
and ability, sulked. But Napoleon paid as little
attention to the advice, the protests and the sulks
as he paid to Josephine's pleadings and his mother's
warnings.

If Napoleon had listened to his mother, he might
have died in the Tuileries, but that is very doubtful.
But it is certainly true that if he had listened to his
mother he would never have slept in the Tuileries.
She was terrified by his glory. She never believed
that it could last. She always anticipated the
disastrous end.

In all that is essential to a man, the Emperor
Napoleon I was an Italian. The Bonapartes were
an ancient Tuscan family with a history dating back
to the first Crusade. Theirs was the fate of many
other noble Italian families, and in 1529 they were
compelled by poverty to emigrate to Corsica.
Napoleon's father, Charles, was a handsome,
clever, weak, genial, amorous lawyer, a disciple
of Voltaire, a writer of light verse, an eighteenth-
century ne'er-do-well. Napoleon said of him that

he was too fond of pleasure to think of his children. He had a small official position as assessor in the French Royal Court at Ajaccio.

In 1764, Charles married Maria Lætitia Ramolinio, who also belonged to an Italian family, emigrated generations before from Lombardy. In her youth, Lætitia was a grave, handsome girl whose appearance is said to have recalled the Mona Lisa. Paoli the Corsican patriot christened her " the rustic Cornelia." She was almost entirely uneducated. She never learned really to speak French. All through her life her outstanding quality was the peasant's thriftiness. She was the mother of many children, and until what was to her the miraculous rise of her son made her greedy, her children's interests were her one interest. Napoleon said of her: " My excellent mother is a woman of brain and heart; to her I owe all my fortune, all the good I ever did."

In 1768, the year before Napoleon's birth, the Corsicans, led by Paoli, rose against the French, and Charles Bonaparte, probably bored by the Ajaccio law court, joined the rebels. His wife, who was *enceinte* with Napoleon, her second son, was with her husband all through a disastrous campaign, suffering every sort of discomfort, on several occasions in danger of her life, always courageous. She had hardly arrived back to Ajaccio when Napoleon was born, on August 15th, 1769, the feast of the Assumption. Charles Bonaparte contrived to retain his assessorship and his small income, but he died of cancer of the stomach on February 24th, 1785, leaving his widow nothing but her children.

When the Revolution broke out, Napoleon had begun his military career, and he and Joseph, during a stay in Corsica, attempted to rally the island to the Republic. But Corsica remained royalist and Lætitia, doubtless recalling her adventures twenty-five years before, had to flee for safety to the mountains with her younger children. " Look, your house is burning," she was told. " Let it burn, we will build a better one," was her stoical reply. On June 11th, 1793, thanks to Napoleon's influence, the whole family crossed to Toulon. There and in Marseilles they lived in great poverty, Napoleon's sisters doing their own washing at the public wash-houses. After the successful siege of Toulon, in 1794, Napoleon moved his mother and sisters, Elisa and Pauline, to Antibes. Elisa was plain, but Pauline was very beautiful, and both of them had been the subject of a great deal of scandalous gossip which reflected on their upbringing and is a curious comment on the influence of their pious Corsican mother. The family story developed at

Antibes. Lucien, always self-willed and idealistic, married the sister of a small inn-keeper, much to his mother's disgust, but Joseph married the daughter of a rich soap-boiler who brought him a dowry of 150,000 francs, much to his mother's satisfaction.

In the autumn of 1795, Napoleon, then twenty-six, passed from obscurity to fame. The " whiff of grape-shot " had made him the Man of Destiny, and he at once began to find positions for his brothers. " The Bonapartes are a clan, and Napoleon is the man of the clan." Before starting for his first Italian campaign, Napoleon married Josephine Beauharnais, without asking his mother's consent as a good Corsican son should have done, and she was furious when she heard of it. She looked to Napoleon to forward the interests of his brothers and sisters. Josephine, a penniless aristocrat, brought him no dowry. She was robbing the clan. Before they had seen her, the whole family, under the mother's influence, hated her, and a real Corsican vendetta was declared which continued till the divorce.

After his marriage and on his way to the army in Italy, Napoleon spent two days with his mother, and a week later she was persuaded to write Josephine a letter that was probably drawn up at a family council, in which she said: "Nothing is wanting to my happiness save the satisfaction of seeing you. Be assured that I feel for you all a mother's tenderness and that I love you as much as my own children." A fine example of humbug.

In the summer of 1797, Mme. Bonaparte went from Marseilles to Montebello to secure Napoleon's approval for the marriage of Elisa, the most capable of his sisters, with Felix Bacciochi. The bride-groom was a penniless Corsican, and Napoleon gave reluctant approval to a marriage that had already taken place in Marseilles. At the same time he told his mother that he had arranged for Pauline to marry Leclerc, an incompetent soldier who was to command the unsuccessful expedition to San Domingo in 1801.

Each of his sisters received a dowry of 40,000 francs. Napoleon, still a soldier of fortune, had done well out of the Italian campaign.

After Pauline's marriage and during the Egyptian campaign, Mme. Bonaparte went to Ajaccio with Elisa and her husband, where she busied herself with family affairs. By the middle of 1799 the Bona-partes were all settled in Paris. Six years before they were penniless. Now they were great and powerful. But Mme. Bonaparte had no belief in the stability of the family fortunes. She hoarded

much of the money that was given her and invested
it in small quantities all over Europe in fear of
what might happen. She was very secretive about
these investments. As early as 1798 she had de-
posited 50,000 francs with a Neapolitan banker and
had lost the whole of it, never saying a word to her
son either of the investment or the loss.

In Paris she lived with her half-brother, soon to
be Cardinal Fesch, in a mansion at the corner of the
Rue Mont Blanc and the Rue Saint-Lazare, having
her own very plainly furnished rooms. She fought
her children's battles, particularly that of Lucien,
whom she loved the most, and she was constantly
denouncing Josephine to her husband. " This
Creole says soft nothings to every man and kisses
every woman instead of attending to her business
of bearing children." To the Corsican a barren
wife was a dishonour to her husband.

In the early months of 1804, shortly before the
proclamation of the Empire, Napoleon and his
mother had a serious quarrel concerning Lucien,
who, against the Emperor's wish, and indeed
against French law, had married a second wife
of whom, not without reason, his brother strongly
disapproved. But his mother was furious with
Napoleon, and she left Paris for Rome, where Fesch,
now Cardinal, was installed at the French Lega-

tion. She was received in the Eternal City with
royal honours, which did not particularly please
Napoleon. He wrote to the Pope on the 22nd
April: " I thank your Holiness for the amiable
things that you say to me in reference to the arrival
of my mother in Rome. The climate of Paris is
much too damp and cold for her. My first physi-
cian advised her to settle in a warm country more
resembling her native land." The fact, of course,
was that she had gone to Italy in a rage.

Napoleon was always generous to his mother.
He had settled a yearly income of 120,000 francs
on her and had paid for the improvements in her
house. He paid Gerard 8,000 francs to paint her
famous full-length portrait. But dearly as she
loved money, money was not enough. She was
angry because she was not given precedence over
Josephine and because of the treatment of
Lucien.

Napoleon was crowned Emperor on December
2nd, and his mother was not at the coronation.
She was, as a matter of fact, always opposed to her
son making himself Emperor. At first she was
more than a little amused by the family quarrels
about titles, but finally she herself succumbed
to the game and made trouble about both title
and precedence. She remained in Italy, staying

with Lucien at Frascati and afterwards with her daughter Pauline at Lucca.

The old lady had grown very jealous. She was jealous of the titles and still more of the money that had been given to her brother and her children. Her sons were princes, her daughters were princesses, but she was nothing. Cardinal Fesch wrote to Napoleon:

" Your mother is ambitious for a title, a settled position. She is distressed that some persons call her Majesty and Empress Mother and that others give her only the title of Imperial Highness which her daughters bear. She is impatient to learn what you have decided upon. She no longer desires to return to Rome. She anticipates that your Imperial Majesty will summon her to Paris before the end of August, the date that she intends leaving Lucca."

Napoleon entirely refused to sanction the title " Empress Mother," since that would have implied that his father was an emperor, which was absurd, and it was finally decided that she should be known as *Mère de sa Majesté l'Empéreur* and that she should be addressed as *Madame Mère*. Her income was raised to 300,000 francs a year, and she never said " Thank you."

She was back again in Paris a fortnight after the

coronation, more fearful than ever. She was certain
that this sort of thing could not last. With it all,
she never lost her dignity. At the first military
parade held after the Emperor's coronation, his
mother was on the balcony of the Tuileries dressed
very simply in black, but looking far more regal than
the over-dressed Josephine. She had now acquired
a stock phrase. When she was flattered on her
son's greatness, she invariably replied in her bad
French, "provided that it lasts." She lived now
in the Hôtel Brienne, which she had bought from
her son Lucien for 600,000 francs.

Soon after her return she was forced by the
Emperor, much against her will, formally to protest
against Jerome's marriage with the American, Miss
Patterson. In his mother's eyes Jerome, like
Lucien, could do no wrong.

Lucien had, of course, remained in Italy. When
Napoleon arranged to go to that country to be
crowned King of Italy in May, 1805, his mother
again strove earnestly to effect a reconciliation
between her two sons. She wrote to Lucien that
Napoleon was anxious to be friends. "Seize the
favourable moment. Do not allow this fine opportunity to escape to reunite yourself to your brother,
but assure your happiness and that of your family.
If you neglect this chance I fear it may be the last

14

that will present itself." Lucien badly wanted to
be a prince and to share his brother's fortunes, but
he refused to give up the woman whom Napoleon
described as "a dishonourable woman who bore
him a child before he had married her, who was his
mistress when her husband was in Santa Domingo."
If Napoleon and Lucien had been reconciled, would
the family have been saved? It was Lucien, a
crafty political intriguer, who had gained the First
Consulship for his brother. He had insight. He
had courage. Could he have contrived to save his
brother from the irreparable blunders of 1813?
This is an interesting speculation that can never be
answered.

Before the Emperor's departure for Italy, Mme.
Mère had been formally granted her title by decree,
and she had been given the place of honour at the
baptism in Notre Dame of Napoleon Louis, afterwards the Emperor Napoleon III, the second son of
Louis and Hortense the daughter of Josephine.
She was given the Dauphin wing of the Palace of
Versailles, but she grumbled at her apartments and
wanted the whole palace. Napoleon's patience
with his family was amazing. His mother was not
satisfied with her apartments at Versailles, so he
bought her the Château du Pont on the banks of
the Seine, for which he paid 214,000 francs, and

another 160,000 francs for its furnishing, besides giving her thirteen pieces of Gobelin tapestry.

There is an interesting contemporary picture of Mme. Mère at this time when she was nearly fifty-five. She had small, perfectly formed feet and perfect teeth. Her eyes were small and black; their expression was always good-natured. She was very fastidious in her dress and, as I have said, strikingly dignified. Her ignorance of French made her very timid, and she was always afraid that she was being laughed at. But she was tactful, and all through her life she retained her shrewdness of judgment. But she grew greedier and greedier and more and more exacting. In 1806, her allowance was raised to 480,000 francs, but she was furious that in the table of precedence of the Imperial family her name was not even mentioned.

In May, she wrote to Napoleon telling him exactly what she expected. She demanded an income of a million, and she wanted it ensured for her by law in case her son should die or lose the throne. The peasant was not lost in the Emperor's mother. This was refused, but as a solatium her son gave her a present of 600,000 francs and twelve more pieces of Gobelin tapestry! At the same time, and probably to please his sister, he heaped lucrative positions on his entirely incompetent uncle, Cardinal Fesch.

In the summer of 1806, Mme. Mère made one further attempt at peace-making between Napoleon and Lucien. She wrote to Lucien—he was still in Italy—" I am destined to pass my life in sadness and desolation; I have finished for ever speaking to you on this subject, and in the future I shall limit myself to deploring in my conscience your disgrace and my own."

In 1807, Mme. Mère was the Mother of Kings. Napoleon was Emperor of the French. Joseph was King of Naples and soon to be King of Spain. Louis was King of Holland. He was Napoleon's favourite brother, an unhappy, dissatisfied man, constantly quarrelling with his wife, Hortense. Jerome, the youngest and stupidest of the family, was King of Westphalia. Caroline, married to Murat, was soon to be Queen of Naples. Elisa was princess in her own right of Piombino and Lucca, two joint principalities with a hundred thousand inhabitants, her husband being a mere prince consort. Her government was entirely successful and commonsensical. She reformed abuses, abolished vexatious taxes, reorganised industry, amongst other things reopening the quarries of Carrara. Elisa was an extraordinarily capable woman who changed her lovers as often as she changed her shift. Pauline alone of the family remained in Paris. Her first husband Leclerc having died, she was married in 1803 to the Prince Borghese, whom she grew to detest, finding consolation with many lovers.

In 1810, the whole of Europe was at Napoleon's feet. Josephine was divorced in December, 1809, much to the delight of Mme. Mère, and the Emperor married Marie Louise of Austria, that dull and fractious lady, on April 1st, 1810. That was his zenith.

But Mme. Mère grew more and more unhappy. The clan had risen to amazing greatness, but its unity was broken. As Emile Ludwig says: " It seems to her that the greatness for which the world envies her family has brought in its train nothing but discord, jealousy, arrogance, ostracism and betrayal. Her thoughts fly back to her native land, where her kindred always formed a united front against other clans. Moreover, her eyes though old are clear-sighted; and she sees that the star of the Buonaparti is paling."

1812 saw the disastrous Russian campaign, and in the spring of 1813 Austria, Russia and Prussia were allied against France. The life of Mme. Mère had begun in trouble, and now, when trouble was returning and her great son was threatened by his enemies and compromised by her weaker sons, she showed herself at her finest. She had been greedy and petty in prosperity. Now she was magnificent. She returned to the mood of Ajaccio, and indeed she needed all her fortitude. In December, 1813, Murat, whom Napoleon had made King of Naples, betrayed his master and made peace with the Austrians, and Mme. Mère never forgave her daughter Caroline, Murat's wife, for the treachery. "If you could not command you should have fought him. It was only over your dead body that your husband should have stabbed his brother, your benefactor, your master."

On March 31st, 1814, Paris surrendered to the Allies. The Napoleonic dream was over, and Mme. Mère was not in the least surprised, nor was she surprised when the men whom her son had made powerful and rich hurried to join his enemies. When his abdication was confirmed, his mother was anxious to stay with him, but he urged her to go to Italy, a journey for which she had already prepared. Marie Louise said good-bye to her and wished her well. "That will depend on you and on your future conduct," was the caustic reply.

It was determined that the Emperor should be banished to Elba, and his brothers and sisters were in terror that they should be sent to Elba too, but Mme. Mère had no such fear. She had se- cured safe-conducts and passports for Nice, where

Napoleon had wished her to go, as well as half a million francs for expenses. It should be said that her income was in arrears and her château at Pont-sur-Seine had been entirely destroyed by the soldiers of the allied armies.

She arrived with her brother Fesch at Rome on May 12th, eight days after her son had landed in Elba. She proceeded at once to realise her possessions. She sold her Paris hotel for eight hundred thousand francs and had all her furniture shipped to Rome, and she at once began to plan to visit her son in Elba, where she arrived with Pauline on August 1st. The Emperor was glad enough to welcome his shrewd old mother. He would have been still more glad to receive Marie Louise and his son. But they never came. Mme. Mère was happy in Elba. There was no longer any reason to fear her son's assassination, a fear that never left her while he was Emperor, and Elba was so like Corsica.

Napoleon escaped from Elba at the end of February, 1815. It was characteristic of his mother that she should advise Lucien: "The Emperor has left with his whole troop, but I do not know for what destination." She hurried back to Italy, where she rejoined Fesch, and with him she sailed for France, where she landed on

May 22nd, nearly two months after the beginning
of the Hundred Days and less than a month before
Waterloo. She did not actually reach Paris until
June 2nd.

Waterloo was fought and lost on June 18th, and
a week later Mme. Mère went to Malmaison to bid
her son a last farewell. There were tears in her
eyes, but neither she nor her son lost their self-
control. "Adieu, mon fils." "Adieu, ma Mère."
And that was all. Three weeks later she started
again for Rome, now simply *Mme. Lætitia Fesch,
veuve Bonaparte.* The Mother of Kings was no
more.

At Rome she was treated with every consideration by the Papal Government, and repaid kindness
by punctilious care to afford no embarrassment.
In 1818, she was much disturbed at the news of
Napoleon's health and wrote a letter to the allied
sovereigns begging for his release. The letter was
not answered. She would have gone herself to
care for him had she been permitted, and she was
righteously indignant at the indifference of Marie
Louise. "Why is my daughter amusing herself
in Italy instead of joining her husband in St.
Helena?" When Napoleon died in 1821, she
wrote again, this time to the British Government,
asking that his body might be brought to Europe.

That request too was refused. She remained in Rome, strong, stubborn, Napoleon's mother. Again to quote Ludwig: " She sits there facing her son's bust, her spirit unbroken, mourning her dead."

She alone of her family had been thrifty and had put by for a rainy day, and in her last years she was continually pestered for money by her sons and daughters. She died in 1836 at the age of eighty-five. Six years before she had had a bad fall which almost crippled her, and she became almost totally blind.

MADAME DE STAËL

IN the year 1755, Edward Gibbon, the future author of *The Decline and Fall of the Roman Empire*, then a boy of eighteen, studying at Lausanne, fell in love with Suzanne Curchod, the pretty and ambitious daughter of a Swiss pastor, and indulged in the common youthful dreams of future felicity. His father, however, a stern English Tory, would not hear of " such a strange alliance," and his son was called home. Gibbon records in his pompous manner: "I yielded to my father; I sighed as a lover; I obeyed as a son."

After Gibbon's return to England, Suzanne went to Paris as the companion of a rich and none too virtuous lady, and in 1764 she married Jacques Necker the Swiss banker, who, Carlyle says, possessed "a taciturnity and solemnity of depth or else of dullness," and who was French Finance Minister in the years before the Revolution. Anne Louise Germaine, Necker's only child, was born in 1766.

Mme. Necker was a rather heavy Swiss intellectual, and her husband was rather depressing. " One felt oneself more stupid in his company than when alone," said Mme. Du Deffard. But Necker was rich and influential, and his wife was something of a lion hunter, and the best and most interesting of the Paris of the years before the Revolution was to be found in her salons. Diderot the philosopher, Grimm, now remembered with gratitude for his collection of fairy tales, and Buffon the naturalist were among her friends. It was a most interesting world in which Germaine spent her girlhood and young womanhood. She was tremendously precocious. When she was eleven, she argued seriously and intelligently with the philosophers. She read, she wrote, she hated play, and her mother stimulated and encouraged her. "Showing her daughter off " was the chief attraction of her literary parties. The result of all this was that at fourteen Germaine had a complete breakdown. She was forbidden to study. She was sent away from Paris, and she escaped from her mother, who resented the illness and, from that time, took only the smallest interest in her only child. When, years afterwards, she was congratulated on her daughter's fame, she said: "She is nothing to what I could have made her."

Rescued by illness from her mother, Germaine

found her father, the stolid financier, who was bored by the intellectuals and who particularly disliked literary ladies. In 1781, Necker fell from power, and a great deal of his new leisure was spent in company with his daughter to the great benefit of them both. Of course they talked politics— everyone did in Paris—but they frivolled and romped as well, and Germaine conceived for her father and for his opinions, Saint-Beuve says, "an enthusiasm which time and death only increased." Under his influence she became a moderate Liberal, desiring for France a constitutional monarchy on the English model, and she remained a moderate Liberal all her life.

The books that most affected Germaine were Rousseau's *La Nouvelle Heloise*, and to a less degree his *Contrat Social*, and Richardson's *Clarissa*. She was a strange mixture of sense and sensibility. In her writing there is constantly what Saint-Beuve has called "an exaggerated pathos." Her judgments were always swayed by sentiment. An utterly unreal melancholy is the note of her fiction. From Rousseau she learned to believe in the "perfectibility" of the human race, and she believed that the business of the politician was to secure social conditions calculated to hasten its attainment. But she never had much faith in the coming of the millennium. Her pessimism is expressed in the poem that begins:

> Mais un jour vous saurez ce qui éprouve le cœur,
> Quand un vrai sentiment n'en fait pas le bonheur.

Rousseau preached the gospel of "back to nature." But nature had small attraction for Germaine. She was always a Parisian, the woman of a great city. "My soul is not rural," she wrote to Mme. Récamier, and in her last years she confessed: "Were it not for the sake of appearances, I would not open my window to see the Bay of Naples, while I would go five hundred miles to talk to a learned man."

There were, of course, many suitors for Necker's daughter's hand, among them William Pitt, who stayed in Paris in 1783, and whose suit was greatly favoured by her mother. But Germaine would not leave France and her father. She admired England, but she had no intention of becoming an English-woman. In 1786, she married the Baron de Staël, the Swedish Ambassador in Paris, a pleasant, good-humoured man, for whom she never professed to have the smallest passionate affection, and whom after a few years she came to detest. The letter she wrote to her mother after her marriage is an amusing example of her exaggerated sentimentality: "To-night I shall not have in my

house the angel that guaranteed it from thunder
and fire. I shall not have her who would protect
me if I were dying, and would enfold me, before
God, with the rays of her sublime soul."

Germaine did not love her husband, but she
loved many lovers. Among the first of them was
Talleyrand, so says prudish but scandal-loving
Fanny Burney, and he was always one of her
most influential friends. Then, after her marriage,
came Louis de Narbonne, who through her influence
became Minister of War in the revolutionary
Government of 1791, and who in 1792 was helped
by her to escape from the guillotine to England.
In addition to Talleyrand, who was nominally
a bishop, and Narbonne, who had a wife, she had
in these years an even more passionate affair with
Matthieu de Montmorency, who had fought in
America with Lafayette, and who was the youngest
member of the Constituent Assembly, the calling
of which heralded the Revolution.

Necker was a popular hero in the early days of
the Revolution, but he soon became suspect and
hurriedly fled to his native Switzerland, " lucky
to reach it alive." His daughter, protected to
some extent by her husband's diplomatic position,
remained in Paris, intriguing with the Moderates,
contriving escape for her friends, listening terror-

stricken to the shouts of the mob on the night of the massacre of the Swiss Guards. Her own life was in danger. Her carriage was on one occasion surrounded by " a furious crowd of old women risen from hell." She was hurried to the Hôtel de Ville, and it was with the greatest difficulty that she obtained permission to leave Paris for Switzerland, where she rejoined her father at Coppet on the Lake of Geneva in September, 1792.

In 1793, Mme. de Staël came to England, where she stayed in a curious colony of French emigrants, among whom were her three lovers, at Mickleham in Surrey. After four months she returned to Switzerland, and in 1794 she met Benjamin Constant, of whom she wrote: " He is the man in the world whom I love the best, the man to whom I cling by every fibre that remains to me of life." Constant was a brilliant, good-looking young man, partly educated in England, as unmoral as he was gifted, and with him she returned to Paris at the end of the Terror. The return was not without its peril. She was known as the friend and associate of aristocratic emigrants. Paris was the very capital of suspicion, and after a few weeks she was denounced in the National Convention and ordered to leave the city. In the beginning of 1796, Germaine and her Benjamin paid a short visit

to Sweden, but Barras, Carlyle's " man of heat and
haste," the lover of Josephine Beauharnais, afterwards to be Napoleon's wife, was her friend, and,
thanks to his good offices, she was permitted to
return to France, having meanwhile written a book,
with the terrible title of *On the Influence of Passion
on the Happiness of Individuals and Nations.* The
"philosopher in petticoats " was soon one of the outstanding figures in the hectic society of the Paris of
the Directoire, the Paris that, under the leadership
of Barras with his scantily clad women, among them
Josephine de Beauharnais and Madame Récamier,
was trying hard to forget the guillotine and the
Place de la Revolution. Germaine was quite as
unmoral as the rest of the Directoire ladies, but
she had infinitely more brains than most of them,
with a tremendous ambition to play a leading part
in the turmoil of French politics.

In the year 1796, Napoleon Bonaparte, a young
man of twenty-seven, returned to Paris after his
supremely successful campaign in Italy, and Mme.
de Staël, then a woman of nearly thirty, met him
for the first time. She has left a description of
Napoleon as he was then:

" His face was thin and pale, but not unpleasing.
Being short of stature, he looks better on horse-
back than on foot. In social life, he has rather

awkward manners, though he is by no means shy.
When he is on the alert, he is a little contemptuous
in his bearing; whereas his natural demeanour is
a trifle common. The contemptuous pose suits
him better. . . . When he is speaking, I am enthralled by an impression of his pre-eminence,
though he has none of the qualities of the men of
the study and of society. If he recounts his
personal experiences, he often discloses the lively
imagination of an Italian. . . . But I always
become aware of a profound irony, which nothing
escapes, neither the sublime, nor the beautiful, nor
even his own fame. . . . . I have known not a few
men of note, some of them savage by disposition,
but the dread with which this man fills me is a
thing apart. He is neither good nor bad, neither
gentle nor cruel. He is unique; he can neither
inspire nor feel affection; he is more and less than
a man."

Germaine was not particularly good-looking.
Her face and figure were both definitely Teutonic,
but she had beautiful hands and piercing black eyes.
Passion was her pastime almost as much as intrigue.
Before she had met Napoleon, many men had loved
her, and she had determined that he should be
numbered among her conquests. This ambition
was quite as much political as amorous. The

Directoire Government was feeble and unpopular. France was yearning for a strong man. Germaine had discussed the situation with her wise friend Talleyrand, and they had agreed that the pale-faced young general, just returned with glory from Italy, might be that man, and if he were to climb to supreme power, Germaine had determined that she would climb by his side.

But Napoleon was not to be caught. He was still entirely in love with Josephine, whom de Staël contemptuously described as " a little insignificant Creole," and he had no liking for over-intelligent women who wrote books and dabbled in politics. From their very first meeting he was openly and definitely afraid of her. Germaine had a reputation for getting her friends into trouble, and it was easy enough to get into trouble in Paris in 1796.

Germaine was not easily repulsed. She chased Napoleon with a will. She wrote him endless letters. Proud as she was generally, she was unaffected by his snubs. But it was little use angling for compliments from Napoleon Bonaparte. " Whom do you think the most celebrated woman in the world ?" she asked him once. " The woman who has brought the most children into the world," was the characteristic Corsican answer.

Napoleon left Paris for the Egyptian campaign

that would have ruined a less lucky commander, and was back again in Paris in 1799 for the Revolution of the 18th Brumaire which made him First-Consul and put him firmly on the road to the throne. Mme. de Staël continued to chase, and Napoleon continued to elude her, and at last she grew exasperated, and at the parties in her well-filled salon she began to talk loudly of the loss of liberty and of the coming tyranny. Joseph Bonaparte, Napoleon's elder brother, advised her to be careful, but she did not believe that the First Consul would dare to take any action against her, and she merely replied in the true Rousseau manner: " I must act according to my convictions." She was bold enough to inspire Constant to an attack on Napoleon in the *Tribunat*, the House of Commons of the Consulate, and this brought a flood of abuse on her head from the well-censored Press. One paper said: " It is not your fault if you are ugly, but it is your fault if you are an intriguer." Another declared that she was fond of writing about morality, " which she talked of without practising, and of the virtues of her sex, which she did not possess." The crowds at her parties began to fall off, and she was warned by Fouché, the Minister of Police, that it would be well if she were to leave Paris for a while. When she returned,

Napoleon refused to receive her. " If only you would show a little good will towards her she would adore you," urged his brother Joseph. " I do not like that sort of adoration. She is too ugly," was the reply.

Germaine was not easily cowed, and she went on talking at the top of her voice. Again she was warned, this time by Talleyrand, to whom she replied proudly and pompously: " Genius is also a power." Then a new book of hers appeared in which she enlarged on the danger of military ambition, and she received a third warning that if she would not leave Napoleon alone, he would assuredly break her.

Mme. de Staël had been brought up a Protestant, and although religion played no part whatever in her life, she had a particularly bitter hatred of the Catholic Church, and she was furious when, in 1801, Napoleon established the Concordat with Rome and went to Mass at Notre Dame on the following Easter Sunday. This was too much for her. Anti-clericalism was part of her Liberalism. She was as anti-clerical as the Freemasons of the Third French Republic or as the modern Spanish republicans.

A year before there was the prospect of peace between Napoleon and the woman whom he feared.

Napoleon had met Necker on a journey through Switzerland, and the old financier had found much to admire in the young dictator. But Napoleon had no use for doctrinaire financiers. He dismissed Necker as " a banker and an idealist," to the mind of this generation a strange combination, and declared that he had contrived the interview in order to obtain employment. To Germaine's " sensibility " such an explanation was intolerable. Her father, she protested, had gone to Napoleon to plead that his daughter might remain in the Paris that she loved. " It was the last time that my father's protecting hand was extended over my life."

Napoleon was scornful and indifferent and now was truckling to Rome, and Germaine, growing bolder, began to plot his overthrow with a junta of disgruntled soldiers, of whom Bernadotte, soon to be Crown Prince of Sweden, was the most distinguished. Napoleon knew all about the plots, but for the moment he held his hand. Then came the publication of Germaine's novel *Delphine*, which grossly affronted the First Consul by eulogising England and defending divorce, which he had recently made illegal in a very proper attempt to improve Parisian morals.

Delphine is almost incredibly dull, as exaggerated as *La Nouvelle Heloïse*, as unreadable as *Clarissa*.

A contemporary critic wrote of it: " Delphine speaks of love in the manner of a Bacchante, of God in that of a Quaker, of death in that of a grenadier, and of morality as a sophist." It is difficult to discover exactly what Germaine intended the moral of *Delphine* to be. Saint-Beuve protests that she intended to present the impossibility of attaining happiness except in the married state, and this is the more remarkable since her deposed and neglected husband had obtained a separation from her in 1798 and died in the year in which *Delphine* was published. The religion of *Delphine*, such as it is, resembles the Unitarianism of Dr. Priestley, one of the noisiest of the English sympathisers with the French Revolution. Germaine's characters talk and talk and talk. They are verbose even on the way to the scaffold. The most interesting thing to be said about the novel is that it enraged Napoleon.

By 1803 he could stand Germaine no longer, and she was formally exiled from France. Emil Ludwig repeats that Napoleon was afraid of her and her works. He himself explained the fear: " She is able to make people think, people who had never learned or who had forgotten how to think." Tyrants have never had any use for women who make men think.

Germaine went to her Swiss home at Coppet, where she was soon joined by Constant, who had again attacked Napoleon in the *Tribunat* and had been shaken " from his clothes like vermin," and from there she went to Germany. Years before Schiller had praised her " exalted reasoning, entirely unpoetical nature," and Germany generally gave her a royal welcome. One of her German admirers wrote of her: " Mme. de Staël is a queen, and all the intelligent men who live in her circle are unable to leave it, for she holds them by a magic spell. She is of middle height, and without possessing the elegance of a nymph is of noble proportions. She is healthy, a brunette, and her face is not exactly beautiful, but this is not observed, for in sight of her eyes all else is forgotten; they are superb; a great soul not only shines in them but shoots forth flame and fire. And always she speaks straight from her heart."

She was received at the German courts. She was courted by the intellectuals, though Goethe was terrified by her loquacity and even Schiller complained that " her only defect is her extraordinary volubility. One must be turned into a listening machine to be able to follow her." And both Goethe and Schiller were openly relieved when she left Weimar for Berlin, where she met the poet Schlegel, another of her many admirers. Wherever she went she carried on her war against Napoleon with witty epigrams, which were repeated from one end of Europe to the other. Always, too, there were love affairs, though Benjamin Constant remained. With him she lived an extraordinary life with violent quarrels and hectic peace-making, from time to time dashing away, and then always dashing back. The qualities of this amazing woman are bewildering. It was said of her: " Her domination over everything surrounding her is inexplicable and yet undoubted. Did she but know how to govern herself, she could govern the world."

Wherever she wandered she yearned for Paris, and Paris was barred to her. That inflamed her venom against Napoleon. Had she been permitted to live in Paris, she might have been an Imperialist. Banished to Germany, she was the ardent Liberal busily stirring up nationalist resentment of French domination. Napoleon naturally hit back. She was surrounded by his spies, and life became so tiresome for her in Europe that she half determined to go to America.

In 1810, she produced a book on Germany, which was suppressed by the French police, and three years later was published in England by John Murray. It was a book that made history. Its effect was to increase the confidence of Germans in themselves, and it is the fact that it was due to Mme. de Staël that the defeat of Jena was finally avenged. Napoleon was still further enraged. His long arm made her Swiss home impossible, and she took refuge in Vienna, going from there to St. Petersburg, of all European capitals the most anti-Napoleon, where she was received by the Emperor Alexander I, the most sincere of Napoleon's royal enemies.

From St. Petersburg she went to Sweden, where her old friend Bernadotte was now Crown Prince, and it was unquestionably again largely due to her that Bernadotte joined the anti-French coalition and fought against his own country. From Sweden Germaine journeyed to London. She was received by the Prince Regent and became a social lion. "In London," says Lieut.-Colonel C. P. Haggard, "she talked and she talked. She preached, she held forth until she lost breath and her hearers lost patience." She again met Byron, whom she described as "the most seductive man in England," but who was as bored as Goethe by her ceaseless chatter. De Staël said of Byron: "I credit him with just sufficient tenderness to destroy the happiness of any woman."

Napoleon always dreaded the influence of the

salons. No woman ever influenced his career, not even his mother. But he had an instinctive fear of women's influence, and this fear was focussed on de Staël. She was, he said, "a dangerous driving wheel which set the salons in motion," and it was certainly de Staël and the salons that largely contrived the alliance that destroyed him and his Empire.

After Napoleon's first abdication, the Bourbons fawned on de Staël, but now that she had won, she would not pluck the fruits of victory. She remained a genuine Liberal and refused to serve the Bourbons. She was, however, permitted to return to Paris in 1814 after an exile of ten years, and it was then said that there were three powers at that time in Europe—England, Russia and Mme. de Staël. Even the Duke of Wellington and Canning paid court to her.

After a few months Napoleon returned, and Germaine wrote to him promising that if he would repay the two million francs which France owed her father, she would in future devote her literary gifts to his cause. The Emperor answered that he much regretted that he was not rich enough to pay her price. Constant made his peace with the man whom he had viciously maligned. But there was another short exile for Germaine.

Then came Waterloo, the second restoration, and incidentally the payment, at long last, of the two million francs by the French Treasury.

In 1811, de Staël secretly married a handsome Italian Swiss called Rocca, who was twenty-two years her junior, and to whom she bore a son. The marriage seems to have been a success, and Rocca always behaved to her with constant consideration and affection.

Mme. de Staël died in 1817. The last years of her life were spent in her old Swiss home, where Byron was one of her visitors and where she wrote her last book, *Considerations on the French Revolution.* She went back to Paris in the spring of 1817 and died there in July. Mr. Francis Gribble says of her: " She wanted to pull wires; she wanted to be wise and witty; she wanted a group of flatterers to hang upon her wise and witty words; but all that was worth nothing unless she could love and be loved."

In his exile at St. Helena, Napoleon said of her: " She was a woman of great talent and great genius. Nor would it be fair to say that she was a bad woman. But she was a disturbing element and had much influence." She had indeed. In Berlin, in St. Petersburg, in Stockholm, in Vienna and in London, almost as it were as a relaxation from her ceaseless love affairs—I have not mentioned one-half of them—she goaded the Corsican's enemies into activity and alliance. Her books reawakened the spirit of nationalism. Her life is one more proof that the pen is mightier than the sword. She was the one woman that Napoleon feared, and he had every reason to fear her.

No one now reads Mme. de Staël. Her place in the history of literature is inconsiderable. But she played her part in the history of Europe. If Napoleon was " The Man," as Mr. Desmond MacCarthy recently wrote, Mme. de Staël was certainly " The Woman."

FLORENCE NIGHTINGALE

IT has almost always happened that the woman
eager to do things in the world has first had to
go out of her home and, like Norah in *The Doll's
House*, bang the door behind her. Few women, and
indeed very few men, have ever succeeded in
carrying a great mission through to success without
having to face bitter family opposition and without
finally having to cast away family ties and entirely
to disregard family prejudice. The foes that have
at the outset to be faced and overcome are the foes
of one's household, and it is eternally true that he
" that loveth father and mother more than Me is
not worthy of Me."

It was inevitable in the social circumstances that
existed in Europe until almost the end of last
century that the family should have been mainly
a prison for women. The determined man was
always able to scale its walls with comparatively
little difficulty. But even while it was generally
accepted that—

this is fixt
As are the roots of earth and base of all;
Man for the field and woman for the hearth:
Man for the sword and for the needle she:
Man with the head and woman with the heart:
Man to command and woman to obey,

the Church always provided one means of escape, one alternative to the home, and it was in the cloister that, relieved from family tyranny, women had always been able to find themselves and to be themselves. St. Teresa was following long precedent and setting famous example when she disregarded her father's tears and turned her back on her castle home at Avila. She was just as much in the necessary mood of preliminary revolt as St. Joan of Arc was when she mounted her horse and rode out of the village of Domrémy. Family ideals, Mr. Shaw has said somewhere, are like the gods of old. They demand human sacrifice. And the woman, convinced that she has been born in the world with a big job to do, has always declined to climb to the top of the pyre.

St. Joan of Arc revolted when she was a mere child. St. Teresa took her vows when she was in her early twenties. Florence Nightingale did not escape till she was a woman of thirty, though the atmosphere of her family prison was infinitely more soul-deadening than the farmhouse of Lor-

raine or the castle in Spain. The Nightingales
were rich Victorians, and some idea of their family
life may be gathered from Rudolf Besier's admirable play *The Barretts of Wimpole Street*, though
Mr. Nightingale was a pleasanter gentleman than
Mr. Barrett, and there was a Mrs. Nightingale to
subject her daughter to the tyranny of tears.

Florence and her sister, who rejoiced in the
terrible name of Parthenope, were well born and
well educated. In the season they came to London
and were taken to highly respectable parties. The
rest of the year was solemnly spent at one or other
of their father's country houses. Every day their
father read aloud the greater part of *The Times*, an
entertainment which Florence came to loathe.
" To be read aloud to," she said, "is the most miserable exercise of the human intellect. It is like
lying on one's back with one's hands tied and
having liquid poured down one's throat." Other
amusements were reading pious books to papa and
mamma, playing the piano, paying visits and sitting around, and as time went on Florence grew more
and more restless and rebellious. She refused to
" settle down." She did not show the smallest
inclination to carry out her mother's dearest wish
and find " some noble-hearted true man, one who
can love her as she deserves to be loved." One

suitor was persistent and not without great attraction for this cultured young woman. Richard Monckton Milnes, afterwards Lord Houghton, was the friend of Tennyson, Emerson and Swinburne, himself a charming poet and incidentally one of the most distinguished defenders of the Tractarians, was a wooer not easily or quickly to be discouraged. But Florence never had any greater intention of marrying than Teresa or Elizabeth had. She had had enough of convention and restriction. "Voluntarily to put it out of my power ever to be able to seize the chance of forming for myself a true and rich life would seem to me like suicide." There was nothing vague about Florence. She had heard her Voices, and their call was as definite as St. Joan's. St. Joan was ordered to raise the siege of Orleans. Florence Nightingale was ordered to cleanse the hospitals of England.

When she at first announced to her family that she was convinced that she had a vocation for sick nursing, they were quite as appalled as St. Joan's father was when he was told that his daughter had a vocation for leading armies to victory. The suggestion that she should be permitted to work for a few months in the hospital at Salisbury aroused the sternest disapproval and was at once forbidden. Hospital patients were common people, not fit for a lady even to know, and hospital nurses were notoriously undesirable. It was because the common people were neglected and because the nurses needed the discipline of a strong hand that Florence's Voices had called her. She had no illusions about the matter. She has recorded that in the early fifties she was told by a head nurse in a London hospital that " in the course of her large experience she had never known a nurse who was not drunken and that there was immoral conduct practised in the very wards."

The need was real. She had no sort of doubt of her capacity. But the door was barred. " I am worse than dust and nothing," she wrote. She was bored to death. She grew ill, she could not sleep, and she was allowed to go for a holiday in Italy, leaving the family behind. Rome and Florence enthralled her, and in Florence she met Sidney Herbert, from whom years afterwards she was to get the invitation to the Crimea. The Rome holiday made the Derbyshire home even more unendurable. Florence was starved. " Women were not supposed," she wrote, " to need food for their heads or hearts. Only their bodies are kept nourished." And now the daughter had become the revolting daughter. She kicked, and kicked hard, against the pricks. The family drawing-room became a place of active torture, a place forsaken by God. At last she contrived to spend some months at an Institution for Deaconesses, where she received rudimentary instruction in what was then the very rudimentary art of nursing. The life was Spartan, the work was hard, the food was of the simplest, but Florence was braced in body and in soul. " This is life. Now I know what it is to live and to love life."

Florence remained with the deaconesses only for some three months. She returned home with the determination to found a similar institution on her own lines and under her own direction, for even more than St. Joan she was Mr. Shaw's " born boss."

In the months that followed, she was busy determining her own peculiar religious beliefs. Her father had been a Unitarian who had become a member of the Church of England because, apparently, of his position in the county, or rather in the counties. Florence herself was more concerned with good deeds than with faith. Miss Irene Cooper Willis, her latest biographer, says: " By the laws of God she meant moral and ethical principles, by acting on which human beings could realise if not a state of perfection on earth, at least something near to it, vastly improved conditions of living." Hers was a " self-made religion," and her

social service was far more the result of the conviction that she was an abnormally capable person
created for abnormally difficult service than that
she was the unworthy instrument of a divine purpose. Florence Nightingale was no saint, for no
one can ever become a saint without first realising
that he is a sinner.

She was growing old, and her hand had not
yet been put to the plough. She was becoming
hungrier and hungrier, for she was still condemned
to comparative inaction. Hitherto her life had
been empty, and she would not pretend that it had
been full. She wrote to her father on her thirty-
second birthday: " I am glad to think that my
youth is past and rejoice that it never, never can
return—that time of follies and bondage, of unful-
filled hopes and disappointed inexperience, when a
man possesses nothing, not even himself."

At the beginning of the next year, 1853, she
stayed for a time in Paris, visiting convents and
hospitals, intent on adding to her knowledge of the
one subject which held her interest. " She is so
thankful to drop being ladylike," wrote one of her
friends, " that she does not even take a cab but
goes by omnibus, which she finds most amusing."
In the summer she was again in London, and at last
she realised her ambition, let it be added in a most

genteel manner, by becoming the superintendent of
" an Institution for Poor Gentlewomen in Illness "
in Harley Street. The Institution was governed
by a committee of ladies whom Florence christened
" the fashionable asses," and whom she dragooned,
bullied and sometimes deceived, always most
properly intent on having her own way. Florence
had left home for good. It was while she was in
Harley Street, hesitating whether or not to accept
the post of nursing superintendent at King's
College Hospital, that the opportunity of her life
arrived. On March 28th, 1854, England and
France declared war on Russia, and the allied army
landed on the peninsula of the Crimea in the following September. On the 20th the Russians were
defeated at the battle of Alma. This prompt
military success was accompanied by what to the
modern mind is the almost incredible neglect of the
wounded. There was no Royal Army Medical
Corps with its trained stretcher-bearers in the days
of the Crimea, only a few decrepit Chelsea Pen-
sioners too feeble to carry the stretchers and so old
that most of them themselves died during the campaign. The wounded, some of whom were lying
on the ground for over two nights, were transported
across the Black Sea to Scutari without the smallest
medical attention, and there was precious little

relief when Scutari was reached. Miss Willis quotes the message from the special correspondent of *The Times* printed on October 12th:

" It is with feelings of surprise and anger that the public will learn that no sufficient preparations have been made for the proper care of the wounded. Not only are there not sufficient surgeons—that, it might be urged, was unavoidable; not only are there no dressers and nurses—that might be a defect of system for which no one is to blame; but what will be said when it is known that there is not even linen to make bandages for the wounded ? The greatest commiseration prevails for the sufferings of the unhappy inmates of Scutari, and every family is giving sheets and old garments to supply their wants. But why could not this clearly fore-seen want have been supplied ? Can it be said that the battle of the Alma has been an event to take the world by surprise ? Has not the expedition to the Crimea been the talk of the last four months ? And when the Turks gave up to our use the vast barracks to form a hospital and depot, was it not on the ground that the loss of the English troops was sure to be considerable when engaged in so dangerous an enterprise ? And yet, after the troops have been six months in the country, there is no preparation for the commonest surgical operations ! Not only are the men kept, in some cases, for a week without the hand of a medical man coming near their wounds; not only are they left to expire in agony, unheeded and shaken off, though catching desperately at the surgeon whenever he makes his rounds through the fetid ship; but now, when they are placed in the spacious building, where we were led to believe that everything was ready which could ease their pain or facilitate their recovery, it is found that the commonest appliances of a workhouse sick ward are wanting, and that the men must die through the medical staff of the British Army having forgotten that old rags are necessary for the dressing of wounds. If Parliament were sitting, some notice would probably be taken of these facts, which are notorious and have excited much concern; as it is, it rests with the Government to make enquiries into the conduct of those who have so greatly neglected their duty."

While the wounded English were left without any sort of attention, the French were being skilfully nursed by devoted nuns, and this striking difference between Protestant and Catholic charity aroused an outburst of angry resentment at home. The War Office could not understand it all. The English War Office always finds it difficult to understand. An abundant supply of doctors had been sent out with an abundant supply of medical stores. Something must have gone wrong. Sidney Herbert, the Secretary for War and Florence Nightingale's old friend, appealed to her for help. She had proved her capacity, she was experienced, she was a lady. He had learned something of her masterfulness during their conversations in Florence. He realised that the task with which she was to be entrusted was immensely difficult, and he was convinced that Florence was the one woman in England capable of carrying it out. The suggestion was made to her on October 14th. On October 21st she sailed with a staff of thirty-eight nurses, fewer than half of whom were really efficient, and it is a curious revelation of the mentality of the governing class in Victorian England that there should have been an outburst of Protestant bigotry because the majority of the nurses chosen by Miss Nightingale were Roman Catholics and Anglo-Catholics. The idea, however, of a comparatively young woman of the leisured classes taking on herself such service for her country aroused the enthusiasm of the nation. How heroic of her to have left her comparatively happy home! They little realised how delighted Florence was to leave it.

When Florence landed at Scutari, Balaclava had been fought, the numbers of the wounded had been

vastly augmented, and the condition of the hospitals was disgusting. There were no basins, no
soap, no towels, no scrubbing brushes, no brooms,
no disinfectants, no knives, no forks, no bedroom
utensils, no clean linen, and no public money to buy
anything. From her own purse and from funds
put at her disposal by *The Times* correspondent,
she secured a moderate supply of necessities, and
then she set herself with overbearing masterfulness,
amazing persistence, and never-failing commonsense to put the house in order. She was opposed
by the obstinate stupidity of generals and military
doctors. She was hindered by the almost incredible
red tape of military organisation. But nothing
daunted her. She foresaw, she prepared, she
ordered, and she conquered. There were four miles
of beds in the hospital in Scutari, and every one was
visited every day by the Lady of the Lamp. She
worked all day and wrote well into the night—
letters of appeal, letters of denunciation. And by
her calm, efficient, unsentimental masterfulness
she gradually, but surely, attracted the devoted
loyalty of the most capable of the men and women
with whom she was associated. The soldiers made
an idol of her. It was impossible that she could
speak to every one of them, but as she passed between the beds " we could kiss her shadow as it fell

and lay our heads on the pillow again, content."
In all probability she would have regarded this as
the sheerest sentimentality, and it is certainly true,
as Mr. Lytton Strachey has insisted in his inimitable
study, that her greatness lay in the fact that she
was an absolutely practical realist, thoroughly
businesslike, thoroughly self-disciplined, never over-
inclined to talk, always ready to act. She did not
suffer fools gladly nor pretend that she did. On the
other hand, she was always calm, she never lost her
temper, she rarely raised her voice. The stupidity
with which she had to contend was never quite conquered, and she was particularly annoyed by the
continuance of the anti-Popish annoyance. One
of her nurses was accused, Miss Willis relates, by a
regimental chaplain of circulating improper literature, the improper literature being a copy of Keble's
Christian Year.

In the spring of 1855, the conditions at Scutari
having been made comparatively decent, Florence
started with a body of nurses to visit the hospitals
in the Crimea itself. Everything was done to
hinder her up to the mean point of orders being
given that she should have no rations. But she had
even foreseen this and had taken an ample supply
of food with her. Her work and influence now
extended far beyond the mere overseeing of a

nursing staff. She had taken on herself the responsibility of seeing that the wounded soldiers were decently clothed. She started canteens, she looked after the soldiers' money and after their wives. She acquired in the army of the Crimea the moral influence that Joan of Arc had in the army of Orleans, and she quite realised that Joan's fate might well be her own. " There is not an official," she said, " who would not burn me like Joan of Arc, if he could." And at last, racked with rheumatism, badly fed, and hopelessly overtired, she herself became seriously ill. She was urged to go home, but she refused. Her work was not done, and she detested the fuss that she knew was being made about her in England. Public affection for her was shown by the starting of a fund for the establishment of a training school for nurses to which the London doctors refused, as a body, to contribute, but to which the Army subscribed nine thousand pounds, most of it in very small sums.

Peace between Russia and the Allies was signed in April, 1856, but it was not until July that Florence Nightingale felt that her work was over. She left Scutari after two of the most strenuous years that woman ever lived.

But she had not come back to rest. She would never forget the horrors of Scutari when she first arrived. She would never forget or forgive the stupidity in high places. " I stand at the altar of the murdered men," she wrote, " and while I live I fight their cause." What had happened should never happen again. Queen Victoria and the Prince Consort became her most valuable backers. On her arrival in England the Queen had sent her an autograph letter in which she said:

" You are, I know, well aware of the high sense I entertain of the Christian devotion which you have displayed during this great and bloody war, and I need hardly repeat to you how warm my admiration is for your services, which are fully equal to those of my dear and brave soldiers, whose sufferings you have had the *privilege* of alleviating, in so merciful a manner. I am, however, anxious of marking my feelings in a manner which I trust will be agreeable to you, and therefore send you with this letter a brooch, the form and emblems of which commemorate your great and blessed work, and which I hope you will wear as a mark of the high approbation of your Sovereign !"

She was asked to Balmoral and had long talks with the Prince Consort, telling him exactly what she had seen and the reforms in the military hospital system that were so obviously necessary. " She is extremely modest," said the Prince. That is

exactly what she was not. She was as immodest
as St. Joan or St. Teresa or Queen Elizabeth.

In alliance with Sidney Herbert, who rightly
shares a good deal of the glory of the achievement
of her lifetime, she set to work persistently to bully
the War Office until it had agreed to the appointment of a Royal Commission on the health of the
Army, with Herbert as its chairman; and in order
that there should be no doubt about the Commission's findings, Florence herself wrote and
printed at her own expense a report which became,
to a large extent, the Commission's report. So
capable was this woman that even the ranks of
Tuscany could scarce forbear to cheer. " She
reasons," said an army doctor, " with a strong,
acute, most logical, and, if we may say so, masculine
intellect." What more could an army doctor say ?
There seems no sort of doubt that the majority of
the Commissioners were indeed in mortal terror of
Florence—most people were—with the consequence
that their report was produced in almost record
time and contained all her own commonsense
recommendations for the improvement of the health
of the Army in peace time and for a proper treatment of the wounded in time of war.

The effect of this incessant driving of the obstinate and the stupid on a woman already wearied by

super-exertions in the Near East led to a complete
breakdown in health, and even she herself began to
fear that she had run her course.   But the publication of the report acted as a tonic, and Herbert's
return to the War Office in the Palmerston ad-
ministration of 1859 made it certain that at least
the greater part of the recommendations would be
put into practice.   Herbert was not a strong man.
He could not stand the strain which Florence put
upon her friends as well as on herself, and he actually died under the harrow, almost his last words
being, " Poor Florence! Our joint work is un-
finished."   His death was a bitter sorrow to her.
She referred to him as " my dear master," but, as a
matter of fact, she was the mistress and he was the
man.   She was far too acute not to know that she
had over-driven him, she was far too honest to
herself not to realise that she was at least partially
responsible for his death.   " If," says Mr. Lytton
Strachey, " Miss Nightingale had been less ruthless,   Sidney Herbert would not have perished,
but then she would not have been Florence
Nightingale."

Until his death the War Office had been her chief
preoccupation.   Her ambition had gone far beyond
a mere reform of the medical service.   She wanted
to reorganise from the garret to the foundation

stone, to instal commonsense in the highest places. In this she did not succeed. The diehards never die.

Herbert's death impelled her interests from the army back to the hospital, and in 1859 she published a pamphlet, *Notes on Hospitals*, which was translated into several foreign languages and had as large a sale in America as in England. Every line of it is instinct with commonsense, and it should not be forgotten that it was written while Mrs. Gamp still flourished. The Nightingale Training School for Nurses was founded and, as Miss Willis says, the nurses trained there formed " a body of apostles " who carried the doctrine of efficiency and hygiene all over the world.

The Indian Mutiny broke out in 1857. Florence volunteered to go out to India to do there what she had done in the Crimea, but her health made that impossible. She was determined, however, that the health of the British soldier in India should receive official consideration, and she wrote a memorandum in which she discussed food and drink, exercises, hygiene, and so on; and in order that the reforms she advocated should be carried out it was she who practically nominated Sir John Lawrence as Viceroy of India when Lord Elgin died in 1863, and for twenty years every Indian Viceroy was constantly in correspondence with her. Never in history has a woman been more completely the power behind the throne. Her biographer says that when the Aga Khan visited her in 1898 when she was quite an old woman, she was disappointed to find that to him sanitation was "unreal and superstitious and religion the only real thing." To her, sanitation was religion.

It was owing to her that in the later years of the last century trained nurses were introduced into workhouse infirmaries and that the sick and the insane were separated from the healthy. She had a lukewarm interest in woman's suffrage, but she realised that, in her time, it was outside the realm of practical politics, and the unpractical never interested her. She was a born, if a beneficent, intriguer. She loved to pull strings from behind the scenes. "I have thought," she said, "that I could work better for others off the stage than on it." Moreover, she infinitely preferred to work with men than with women, and, like St. Teresa, she found men far more loyal to her than women. For her own sex she had something like contempt: "Women crave for being loved, not for loving; they scream out at you for sympathy all day long. They are incapable of giving any in return."

17

It was characteristic of Florence Nightingale
that she was opposed to the registration of nurses,
which was not actually attained until some years
after her death, and this was largely due to the fact
that she had never had to earn her own living, and
that she had come to regard nursing as a vocation
and not as a profession. Sympathy indeed was
never her strong suit. Her vision was very clear.
She saw along straight lines, but she never attempted to understand when she was opposed or
when she was disobeyed.

There is a striking difference in both the tempera-
ments and the methods of St. Teresa and Florence
Nightingale, the two most famous women reformers
in history. Tact was St. Teresa's great quality.
She was a very artful diplomat. She knew exactly
how to twist dignitaries round her finger. Florence
Nightingale knew nothing of tact, and diplomacy
would probably have struck her as rather mean.
She drove, she terrified, she conquered by the sheer
force of a most pugnacious personality.

Honours came to her in her old age. She was a
great national figure. The Order of Merit was bestowed on her shortly before her death. She never
lacked friends and admirers, and yet long before
her faculties began to wane she was fundamentally
a very lonely woman in her house in South Street,

Mayfair, and with all her superb achievement she does not seem to have been a very happy old woman.   Here again is a striking contrast, for St. Teresa, worn out and suffering bitter pain, died serene and content.

CATHERINE BOOTH

THE creation and the swift rise into popularity
of the Salvation Army in the last quarter of
the nineteenth century makes one of the most per-
plexing chapters in the modern history of religion.
In an age when revealed religion was threatened
by the widening of knowledge and when its defenders were straining to prove that there was
nothing really antagonistic between modern
knowledge and the Christian faith, a new development of Protestantism swiftly attained a vast
popular following, not by placating the intellectuals, but simply by ignoring them. The Salvation Army was, from the beginning, designedly unintellectual. It had the same complete contempt
for the wisdom of this world as St. Francis of Assisi
had; but, unlike the Franciscans, who became intellectual in the course of a generation and famous
for scholarship in less than fifty years, after its fifty-
four years of existence the Salvation Army remains,
as it was created, as fundamentalist as the Baptists
of Tennessee. The theology of its founders was

based on an uncritical reading of Holy Scripture, and the adherents of the Army have never been permitted the smallest individual freedom in the interpretation of the inspired Word. The Army has indeed always claimed infallibility with a far greater rigidity and a far smaller measure of intelligence than Rome. Its founder accepted the extreme Protestant view of the inspiration of the Bible, and this view was set out in formulas to which the members of the society are obliged to profess complete acceptance. The "saved soldier" must believe what he is told and must do what he is told. His not to reason why.

General Booth's idea of a religious society that should be military in its discipline and its direction had of course been anticipated by both St. Ignatius of Loyola and by St. Teresa. To these saints, as to General Booth, humanity appeared threatened by the forces of the evil world, against which must be pitted the discipline of devoted soldiers of the Lord. St. Ignatius demanded from the members of the Society of Jesus unqualified obedience and unqualified self-sacrifice. When a man becomes a Jesuit, his individuality is in a sense lost in the life of his community, although, as a matter of practice, his individual qualities are carefully cultivated and developed for the benefit of the community and for the mission which he has undertaken. That is the genius of the Society of Jesus. In no other community have obedience and self-development existed so triumphantly together.

I do not suppose that, when he founded the Salvation Army in 1878, William Booth was particularly conversant with the story of St. Ignatius. He would probably have been more than horrified if he had been told that he was founding a society on the Jesuit model, and of course the statement would only be partially true. The basic conceptions, however, were the same, just as Mr. Booth's sense of responsibility for the rescue of the poorest, the most helpless and the most degraded had high and noble precedent in the achievements of the followers of St. Francis.

The curious thing about the Salvation Army is that, while professing the most complete devotion to the personality of Christ, it rejects, almost without a thought, all those institutions which He Himself devised for the winning of the world. Franciscans and Jesuits had gone into the byways of Europe and into the pagan lands of Asia, Africa and the Americas, carrying the symbol of the Cross. The Salvation Army exchanged the Cross for a drum. It attaches no sort of importance to the

Sacraments. In common with all the Protestant
sects, the Army would naturally reject the doctrine
of baptismal regeneration, the belief that by the
Sacrament of Baptism the individual becomes a
member of the Catholic Church. But Baptism
as the rite of entrance into the society is honoured
by almost all Protestants, and, except for the
Quakers and the Salvation Army, they all attach
reverent importance to Holy Communion. Why
the Booths elected to cut themselves off from the
common practice of Christendom in so far as the
Sacraments were concerned, I do not in the least
understand. It is not to be denied that, apart
from their mystical significance and symbolic
suggestion, the Christian Sacraments possess a
singular and appealing beauty, and this is as true
of a solemn Communion Service in a Scottish
Presbyterian church as of High Mass in a Catholic
cathedral. Perhaps it was the beauty that caused
the rejection, for just as the Salvation Army is
intentionally unintellectual, so it is also intentionally unæsthetic. Its founder stripped worship
—I do not think deliberately, but from a curious
warped mentality—of every vestige of beauty.
The Salvation halls were at the beginning, and
remain, monuments of ugliness, bare, ill-coloured,
unattractive. The uniforms, designed both for

men and women, are magnificently successful in concealing prettiness and emphasising the qualities of the plain. The hymns are mainly doggerel, the tunes are mainly noise. The Army has developed the instinctive Puritan hatred of all beauty, to a greater extent even than the well-to-do Protestants of the Victorian era with their ghastly wax flowers and antimacassars. The Salvation Army has never learned the great truth that, in Dean Inge's words, " the vision of God should appear to us as a triple star of truth, beauty and goodness." In another place the Dean says: " Beauty is the chief mediator between the good and the true: and that is why the great poets have been also prophets." The Salvation Army is eager enough for truth. It claims that it possesses fundamental truth. I would not question that it has had its prophets, but it has never heard the singing of the poets. It has, as it would seem, found God in the earthquake and the tempest, while the still small voice has never reached its ear.

In his autobiography, General Bramwell Booth claimed Mr. Bernard Shaw's authority for rating Salvation Army music as of high artistic excellence. My experience does not justify the claim, but it may be admitted that General Booth agreed with St. Francis that " musical instruments appointed

of old for God's praise have been converted by
man's lust into means of giving pleasure to their
ears." Mr. Nicholson suggests that to St. Francis
music " had its beginning and its end in God."
Again doubtless General Booth would have agreed.
It seems a pity that he did not credit Divinity
with finer taste.

No one can question the reality of the conversions achieved by the Salvation Army, though
how permanent and how fundamental the conversions are is another matter. Through the
Army's ministration, drunkards have certainly
become sober and thieves have become honest,
and no one can have even a slight acquaintance
with the membership of the Army without recog-
nising that it often encourages a charm of character,
sometimes tempered by an over-cocksureness, that
is the consequence of complete certainty of attaining heavenly bliss. Several times during my
life I have had personal relations with leaders of
the Salvation Army, and, with the exception of
the first General, who seemed to me on the two
occasions when I talked to him a rather terrifying
old gentleman, I have found them singularly
courteous and modest, with an obviously considerable measure of that serenity which is frequently
the possession of the religious and is rarely to be

found in the world. There is, as it appears to me, every reason to believe in the reality of their religious experience, for ultimately, despite the admitted danger of pragmatism, faith finds its test in character. Admitting that with all the noise and with all the rant, the Salvation Army has developed and doubtless is still developing characteristically Christian virtues, the question has to be faced whether or not the result has been achieved by the rejection of the good things of this world, by the contempt for thought and for beauty as well as by the honest attempt to avoid all that is more commonly regarded as evil.

Booth and his early followers were as impressed as the early Christians were impressed by the cruelty and wickedness of the world. They were convinced that unless mankind suffered a fundamental change of heart it would most assuredly be eternally damned. And in view of this conviction it may have been true for them, as Mr. Chesterton says of the primitive Christians, that " they had to go into the desert where they could find no flowers or even into the caverns where they could find no stars." To them everything that was worldly was sinful. A symphony concert was as sinful as a beanfeast. The Royal Academy exhibition was literally (many art critics have had the same conviction) the creation of the devil. The theatre stood at the mouth of the pit, and, forgetting the exploits of David before the Ark of the Covenant, it was as sinful to dance as it was to drink.

All this may sound very silly, but, as a matter of fact, considering the task to which William Booth put his hand, it was extremely long-sighted. In the middle years of the last century, that era of fat Victorian prosperity, religion played a large and most respectable part in an essentially irreligious society. The decent citizen would no more have thought of avoiding church-going on Sunday morning than he would of avoiding the paying of his rates or of keeping his servants in their right place. But he always went to church in a top hat. That was his easy, though perhaps rather uncomfortable, way of showing his respect for the Almighty. Religious formalism was being challenged within the Church of England by the Tractarian Movement long before Booth began his mission, and in a manner which he would certainly not have understood. With a righteous impatience of convention and an extraordinarily vivid sense of a mission, he was outraged by an equally deadening formalism in the societies which have now come to be called the Free Churches.

Booth's great discovery was that real religion can never be quite respectable, and that was the great discovery of St. Francis. Whatever else they may have done, the early Franciscans certainly made a joyful noise before the Lord. So long as a man is content to live within the restrictions of traditional convention, regulating his life by the prejudices of his neighbours, so long will he be cutting himself off from the Kingdom of Heaven. " Even those who have lost sympathy with Catholicism cannot help feeling that it is a religion for a gentleman," says Dean Inge. That is true, but there is abundant evidence that Catholicism is also a religion for a cad, although it generally makes the cad into a gentleman. Booth knew as little and cared as little about gentlemen as Charles Dickens himself, but he knew a good deal about cads and he cared a great deal for them. It was their souls that he wanted to be saved. Dean Inge is impressed by the " dignity and calmness " of Catholic piety. Booth had no dignity, and he was a human tempest. Respectability and dignity are by no means the same thing. But if a man cannot retain his dignity without becoming respectable, then he had much better not be dignified. It is certainly true that no man, hide-bound in the bonds of respectability, ever carried through a great mission.

In the whole history of the world, no man and no woman has ever achieved anything worth achieving without setting Mrs. Grundy by the ears. The first of the Booths was narrow-minded, fanatical, ignorant and prejudiced. But he did care, and he cared just for those people for whom the really respectable individual never has any care at all. There is a great saying of the late Frank Weston, Bishop of Zanzibar, so magnificent that I quote it here with some hesitation. He said in his last speech at the Anglo-Catholic Congress in the Albert Hall in 1924:

"But I say to you, and I say it with all the earnestness that I have, if you are prepared to fight for the right of adoring Jesus in His Blessed Sacrament, then, when you come out from before your tabernacles, you must walk with Christ, mystically present in you, through the streets of this country, and find the same Christ in the peoples of your cities and villages. You cannot claim to worship Jesus in the tabernacle if you do not pity Jesus in the slum. . . . It is folly, it is madness, to suppose that you can worship Jesus in the Sacrament and Jesus on the throne of glory, when you are sweating Him in the bodies and souls of His children. . . . You have your Mass, you have your altars, you have begun to get your tabernacles. Now go out into the highways and hedges, and look for Jesus in the ragged and the naked, in the oppressed and the sweated, in those who have lost hope, and in those who are struggling to make good. Look for Jesus in them; and, when you have found Him, gird yourself with His towel of fellowship and wash His feet in the person of his brethren."

The Booths had the spirit of the great Catholic bishop when they went down into the murky streets of Mile End to discover, in their own phrase, " Jesus in the mud."

The conversion of the degraded, the unhappy and the troubled, which was the Booths' mission, was achieved partly by terrorism, the penitent being lashed into agony for his sins. General Booth once recorded in his diary: " Two souls weeping very bitterly: I never saw persons in deeper distress. From about eight till half-past ten they wept incessantly." But sympathy and understanding were not lacking, and it is well to remember that St. Francis was convinced that conversion with the consequent salvation was a matter of the emotions and not of the intellect. Mr. Nicholson says in his *The Mysticism of St. Francis*:

" It may well be that ultimately all conversion and all spiritual influence are a result of a strong and active current of love directed on the person by whom conversion is experienced, and although love may not necessarily be rendered impossible by intellectual activity, it is not, at any rate, an essential or natural part of it. It is impossible to love with the intellect—possible, perhaps, only to appraise with it—and the vital change of life which is called conversion is therefore outside the sphere of its influence. On this St. Francis insisted with unremitting force. He pointed out that the brethren were in danger of believing that they were filled with devotion and illuminated with the knowledge of God because of their understanding of the Scriptures, while, as a matter of fact, they would remain cold and empty within, and be unable to return to their pristine energy of prayer because of the time they had given to intellectual pursuits. He insisted on the danger of appropriation by such brethren of the results of their preaching—the belief, that is, that the credit was due to their own skill instead of to the grace of God—and explained to them in words that they could not mistake that the people whom they believed to have been converted by their own knowledge had, as a matter of fact, been moved by the prayers of the simpler brethren who knew nothing of what they had done."

As it seems to me, the weakness of the Salvation Army is that the realisation of the vast areas of neglected suffering, with the conviction that the suffering can be mitigated and the sorrow can be turned into content by the action of religion, brought with it an unpleasant contempt for those religious bodies which seemed to its leaders to have sorely neglected their duty, and a vast measure of spiritual pride because at last, in face of great difficulties, they had taken on the job. The seventeenth-century Puritan denunciations of priests and priestcraft were repeated with particular vehemence from the Salvation Army platforms. They were the chosen people; alone they were wielding the sword of the Lord and of Gideon. Outside their ranks and among Christians whom they described as " nominal " was nothing but unreality, cowardice, worldliness and false doctrine. " The obtuseness, the indifference and heartlessness of professed Christians," wrote Mrs. Booth, " is the greatest trial of my life," though, in another place, she grudgingly admitted that " many savages and Catholics have rejoiced in the consciousness of pardon."

The Salvationists are the chosen people. They are saved, and they are taught that they may become holy in this earthly life. Their religion is literally their life. The Army demands not a partial, but a complete loyalty from its adherents.

The Salvationist is expected to spend his entire leisure time in the Army's service. It is his business in life to secure the conversion of his friends and acquaintance. He is not to question instructions, he is not to bother about doctrine, he is to believe and to act exactly as he is told. Beauty is shut out of his life. Too much knowledge is regarded as a dangerous thing. And, with all this, in manifold cases he develops sincere sympathy with misfortune and a capacity for genuine self-sacrifice that must commend unqualified respect.

In the beginning of every movement that has changed the lives of men and women and affected the development of society, there is one great gifted personality. I am convinced that the personality that made the success of the Salvation Army possible was not William Booth the autocrat, with his large measure of commercial genius, but his wife Catherine, who, as her writings prove, was a very genuine modern mystic. No religious revival in the history of the world has ever occurred without the inspiration of a genuine mysticism. There are passages in Mrs. Booth's writings comparable to the record of the soul experiences of St. Teresa and St. John of the Cross. For example:

" To love Thee with all my heart is my desire. I do love Thee, but I want to love Thee more. If

Thou smile upon me, I am infinitely happy though deprived of earthly happiness more than usual. If Thou frown upon me, it matters not what I have beside."

"Lay your head on His bosom and draw by a closer communion precious secrets of future service. Rest under His shadow and learn more and more to trust His love."

I could quote many similarly beautiful passages.

She was born on January 17th, 1829, the only daughter of a family of five. Her father was a Methodist preacher, her mother was a stern Puritan who refused to permit her daughter to learn the French language because of her horror of French infidel and impure literature. The cloud over her childhood was the fact that her father, who was a coach-builder as well as a preacher, lost his enthusiasm for religion, though, as a sort of compensation, he became an enthusiast in the teetotal agitation of the thirties of last century. Catherine must have been rather a strange child. Long before she was in her teens, going to religious meetings was her chief interest. She read Butler's *Analogy* and the *Pilgrim's Progress*, though she admitted "a strong antipathy to the Calvinistic tendency of some of its teachings." When she was fifteen, an attractive young man proposed to her, but she rejected his

advances because when they went together to
chapel " he would be sketching pictures on the pew
in order to divert my attention." In her diaries,
written before she was twenty, there is a series of
striking passages suggesting the real mysticism of
the girl's character, but with it, even in these early
days, is a rather repellent " smugness."

Mrs. Booth was one of the earliest protagonists of
women's rights. She was not in the least interested
in women being permitted to vote, but she was
determined that women should be permitted to
preach.

William Booth, who was born in the same year as
his wife, first met her when they were both twenty-
two. On this occasion the founder of the Salvation Army delighted her guests with a recitation of a soul-stirring poem called *The Grog Seller's
Dream*. The recitation was followed by an argu-
ment as to whether or no the Bible permitted the
consumption of alcoholic liquor. The friendship,
thus auspiciously begun, ripened into affection
within the next year. The love letters, printed in
Mr. Booth-Tucker's elaborate biography of his
mother-in-law, are extraordinary documents. Both
the man and the girl were absorbed in religion and
both had an odd priggish self-satisfaction. For
instance, she wrote to him: " I find that the pleasure

connected with pure, holy, sanctified love forms no exception to the general rule. The very fact of loving invests the being beloved with a thousand causes of care and anxiety which if unloved never exist." But Catherine had a large measure of commonsense shown when she wrote to her fiancé: " Don't sit up singing till twelve o'clock after a hard day's work. Such things are not required by either God or man." I should hope not !

In another letter she warned him against ambition and urged him to a particularly Spartan life. At this time he was apparently preaching every evening, and she advised him to get up at six o'clock in the morning and convert his bedroom into a study till breakfast-time ! Some unwise friend suggested that Mr. Booth should take a little port wine, and Catherine was most indignant. " I abominate that hackneyed but monstrously inconsistent tale, a teetotaler in principle but obliged to take a little for my stomach's sake."

The Booths were married at the Stockwell New Chapel on June 16th, 1855. Mrs. Booth's married life was to last thirty-five years, and she was the mother of three sons and five daughters, all of whom inherited her enthusiasm if none of them had quite her qualities or quite her distinction. When she married him, Booth was a wandering

Methodist evangelist, with much the same gifts as the Gipsy Smith of a later day; and it is hardly to be denied that it was the influence of his wife, infinitely his intellectual superior, that filled him with self-confidence and stimulated his ambition to break away from the Methodists and create an organisation of his own. In 1860, Mrs. Booth began her career as a public speaker. Seventy years ago it was still the accepted convention that women should be seen and not heard, and a woman in the pulpit was still so much of a novelty that the services that Mrs. Booth conducted were advertised by posters with the heading, " Come and hear a woman preach."

Her reported speeches suggest an intensity of feeling and an obvious sincerity not always apparent in evangelistic discourses and a literary form which in such discourses is extremely rare. Her eldest son said that his father made the Army, but that his mother " thought out the why and wherefore of it all." He wrote:

" She combined practical sense with deep mysticism. She was aggressive and yet saintly, a teacher of holiness and yet—what is not always true of such teachers—an evangelist turning many to righteousness, some of them from the very depths of sin and despair. She was a social reformer, and

before her indignation many a vested interest
quailed, but none was more tender than she in
dealing with a soul." For twenty-five years
Mrs. Booth preached almost every Sunday, and
often several times during the week. But she never
ceased to be a devoted wife and mother. In one of
her letters to her husband she signed herself " Your
faithful, joyful, loving little wife." She was always
that.

Her children were brought up in an atmosphere
of the most extreme Puritanism. They were
never allowed to go to children's parties. Parties
were worldly. They were not permitted to have
many friends. Friends were dangerous. No novel
was ever allowed within the door. Reading fiction
was a waste of time. She refused to allow her
eldest daughter to go to a good school. She wrote:

" This deadly rage for education ruins tens of
thousands. It is as rank as idolatry, as the worship
of Baal, and God is as jealous of it, and as angry
with it, and will have no more to do with it ! Look
at the ministry. It is an *educated* ministry !
Perhaps you say that they put it in the place of the
Spirit. This fact shows the *danger there is of doing
this*. It is well known in Methodism that hundreds
of young men have gone into their colleges like
flames of fire, *soul-winners* ! But they have gone

to be taught Latin and grammar, etc., and in numberless cases they come out the devil's charred sticks! How is this? Does it not look as if there were something antagonistic between learning and godliness? Does it not prove the great danger of setting the heart on learning and forgetting where the strength for usefulness really lies? How is it that all great soul-savers, even highly educated men, have invariably thrown aside their studies when they have given themselves up to soul-winning?"

Absolute obedience was demanded. And yet with it all and despite the fact that father and mother were often away preaching all over the country, the Booth children seem to have been quite happy children, who adored their mother. They were certainly little prigs, but they were quite happy, pleasant little prigs.

They were brought up in the habit of what must generally be a most unwholesome introspection. From their babyhood they were constantly talking and thinking of their souls. "How is your soul? Better? I hope so," wrote one of her sons to his elder sister. Mrs. Booth denounced "auricular confession and other Popish errors," but she was insistent on the need for self-examination that is the prelude to soul confession and to the Wesleyan

281 CATHERINE BOOTH 281

custom, followed in those days by Dr. Buchman's
adherents, of the public confession of sins. She
wrote:

" There can be no doubt that the class meeting,
as originally intended by Wesley, was an excellent
arrangement, but the mere asking of empty
questions as to how a person is getting on, and the
leaving them to answer by the platitudes usual on
such occasions, is to daub them with untempered
mortar, and to lead them forth in the way of hollow
profession and uncertainty. Pointed questions
should be put, such as, Have you enjoyed private
prayer during the week? How far have you been
enabled to obey the precepts of Jesus Christ in
dealing with your family or your business? Have
you maintained a conscience void of offence toward
men as well as toward God in these matters?
Have you faithfully made use of your opportunities
for doing good? How many have you spoken to
about their souls? Have you succeeded in leading
anybody to decision for salvation or consecration?
Have you practised any self-denial in order to
extend the Kingdom of Christ?

" Such questions pressed home with the aid of
the Holy Spirit would compel confession, and in-
volve a repentance and reconsecration productive
of real results. But of course questions of this

kind presuppose that those who ask them are themselves living up to the standard which they set before others, and this, alas, is too often not the case !"

Mrs. Booth had many magnificent qualities, but she had no glimmering of a sense of humour, and she had a grave suspicion of people who could make jokes. " Be watchful against levity," she wrote. " C—— is a good devoted fellow, but naturally an incorrigible joker. It may not hurt him much because it is his nature, but it will hurt you if you give way to it. It hurts nearly everybody. Don't descend to buffoonery."

This entire lack of a sense of humour encouraged the self-satisfaction to which I have referred, for a sense of humour brings with it a sense of proportion, and the man and woman who have learned to laugh at themselves and at the world are never likely to take themselves over-seriously or to exaggerate their own distinction or their own goodness. It would be untrue to say that Mrs. Booth gloried in her own righteousness. There is the never-failing acknowledgment of divine guidance and mercy. But she had the very comforting certainty that divine grace was conspicuous in the Booth family. In 1861, in a letter to her mother, she said of her husband: " He is now on full stretch for holiness," and a few days later she claims the same thing for herself. " 'Then,' said he, 'are you not holy ?' I replied with my heart full of emotion and with some faith, ' Oh, I think I am.' " I suggest that neither St. Teresa nor St. Francis, St. Augustine nor St. Thomas, nor even our Lady herself, ever had any such conviction.

It was after her death that General Booth started on his social campaign with the publication of *In Darkest England : The Way Out.* But his wife had a well-developed social conscience. She was freely anti-militarist. She wrote after the rejoicing for the capture of Sebastopol:

" I cannot enter into the spirit of the victory.. I picture the gory slain and the desolated homes and broken hearts attending it, and feel saddened. What a happy day will it be for the world when all *Christians* shall protest against war, when each poor mistaken Peter shall have heard Jesus say, ' Put up again thy sword into its place, for all they that take the sword shall perish with the sword '! What a fearful prediction, if it applies to *nations* as well as to individuals ! And hitherto it *has* been fulfilled in the history of the world. If it is yet to be fulfilled in our history, what will be our fate as a people ?"

She had a loathing for the vulgar adoration of

money. She had an intense sympathy with the poor. She denounced injustice, inequality and cruelty. " The man whom Jesus Christ consigned to a hopeless perdition was he who made long prayers and at the same time devoured widows' houses, or whose barns were filled with plenty while Lazarus lay covered with sores at his gate."

Mrs. Booth died after a long and intensely painful illness endured with splendid courage and patience. Almost her last words to her family were: " I will meet you in Heaven," which may be compared with Cardinal Manning's, " It is but a little time, and we shall all keep Easter in Heaven."

" One half of Mrs. Booth's mission," says her son-in-law, " consisted in resurrecting the buried talents of her sex, the other half in humanising the spiritual." She was a mystic, a great speaker, a very courageous crusader.

I am compelled to the comparison of the life of Catherine Booth with the life of St. Teresa. Both women lived with a high and mighty purpose, but while Mrs. Booth was characterised by the most extreme individualism, in St. Teresa there was the acknowledgment of authority with the never-failing purpose of persuading authority to consider new ideas and to sanction new developments. In St. Teresa there was a serenity and a humility not

to be found in Catherine Booth, with her tremendous conviction that only her family and its
followers were the really faithful and the really
efficient servants of the Most High, that indeed the
Booths were the Pope and the Ecumenical Councils
rolled into one.

THE END